EIGHT KEYS
TO
SPIRITUAL
AND
PHYSICAL HEALTH

by Frank Marzullo

with Nina Snyder

INSPIRATIONAL PUBLISHERS

4th Printing, 1989

ISBN 089-221-092-3
Eight Keys to Spiritual and Physical Health
© 1982 by Frank Marzullo
Printed in the United States of America

DEDICATION

This book is dedicated to those saints of God whose lives have been used by Him to display His power and works, and whose lives form the illustrations used in these pages. It is further dedicated to those who are in need of a special touch by the Holy Spirit, and who will recognize and seek this touch as a result of reading this book. I also acknowledge the dedication, love, and work that my daughter, Nina Snyder, has put into the writing, transcribing, and typing of this manuscript. Most of all, however, I would like to dedicate this book to one who has been my constant source of encouragement, my closest friend, my partner in travel, ministry, as well as life—my lovely wife, Evelyn.

FOREWORD

In the body of Christ there is need for a greater manifestation of the gifts of the Holy Spirit. Wherever I go, I see a tendency for people to be mere spectators, letting someone else move in ministry. I believe that God is saying to the Church today: "Participate!" Be a part of the Church. Find out what your gift is and operate in it. Our loving Father has provided everything that we need in this life to be overcomers. As members of the body of Christ, each of us has been called to a particular function or ministry. When we receive the fullness of the Holy Spirit, we can more easily participate and walk in that ministry. Everything has been prepared for us. The only thing we have to do is to present ourselves to the Lord as a living sacrifice and commit ourselves to His service.

Jesus came to destroy the works of darkness: sickness, sin, and all that the cankerworm has eaten up. He described His ministry in Luke 4:18, quoting the prophet Isaiah:

> The Spirit of the Lord God is upon me, because the Lord has anointed me to bring good news to the afflicted; He has sent me to bind up the brokenhearted, to proclaim liberty to captives, and freedom to prisoners. (Isa. 16:1)

Jesus announced that His ministry included salvation, deliverance, and healing. As He walked through the earth, what He was sent to do, He did: He saved; He healed; He cast out demons. Then, He exhorted His disciples to:

> "Go into all the world and preach the gospel to all creation. He who has believed and has been baptized shall be saved; but he who has disbelieved shall be condemned. And these signs will accompany those who have believed: in My name they will cast out demons, they will speak with new tongues; . . . they will lay hands on the sick and they will recover." (Mark 16:15-18)

Once we have experienced the demonstration of God's power, we relate to people and circumstances according to that experience. If you have been healed, you gain confidence to pray for someone else's healing. When you have experienced deliverance, your faith rises and you have the confidence to minister deliverance to others. "Freely you received, freely give" (Matt. 10:18). As the Word of God states, signs should be following those who believe. We must ask ourselves why these signs are not manifested in the Church today by all who claim to be believers.

PREFACE

Christians of this generation have neglected to arm themselves against the wiles and snares of the devil, but not without great consequences. In a day when evil abounds and the works of darkness are advertised and glorified worldwide, we are sadly ignorant of the devil's nature, his power, his devices, and his overall opposition to God and God's creation. It is vital that we comprehend not only the devil's strength, but also his limitations and our authority in Christ over him.

Rev. Frank Marzullo has worked in the deliverance and healing ministry for over fourteen years. He has held many services at Good Shepherd Lutheran Church in North Miami, Florida, and we have seen many miracles here through his ministry.

Frank's book is a long-awaited contribution to this much-needed aspect of Christian ministry. It will bring enlightenment, and understanding as well as power to your Christian walk. For that reason I recommend to the reader, Frank's experienced teachings which are firmly founded upon the Scriptures.

Rev. Robert E. Barber
Good Shepherd Lutheran Church
North Miami, Florida

CONTENTS

Scripture quotations are from the New American Standard version of the Bible, except as otherwise noted.

ONE
ANALYZING
THE PROBLEM

We have discovered that the ministry gift most needed in the body of Christ is discerning of spirits. This would enable one to properly diagnose the nature and cause of a problem and to know how to deal effectively with it. When someone comes with a problem, it is vital to know if this problem is of a physical or spiritual nature. If it is physical, then healing is needed. If it is a condition brought about by a demonic presence, then deliverance should be administered first, followed by prayer for healing if that is also indicated. If it is a problem of the willful carnal nature of man, then repentance is needed. A deliverance should be conducted only after seeking the presence of the Holy Spirit who should be invited into the life of the one being delivered after the demons have left.

The next thing to discover in analyzing the problem is the work of the cross in the individual's life as expressed in his vertical and horizontal relationships; the vertical, meaning his relationship with God, and the horizontal, his relationships with others.

> "'You shall love the lord your God with all your heart, and with all your soul, and with all your mind.' This is the great and foremost commandment. And a second is like it, 'You shall love your neighbor as yourself.' On these two

commandments depend the whole Law and the Prophets."
(Matt. 22:37-40)

The one who ministers should determine if the needy individual, (hereafter referred to as "the brother") is truly saved. Has there been any fruit of repentance? Is there any evidence of a new life? "Therefore if any man is in Christ, he is a new creature; the old things passed away; behold, new things have come" (2 Cor. 5:17). If there is evidence in the brother's life that his past profession of faith was verbal only and did not touch his heart, the minister must lay a new and scriptural foundation, call the sinner to repentance, and lead him to the cross of salvation as if he had never before heard of the Lord Jesus Christ.

If the brother is still repeating the old patterns of sin as in the days before his conversion, find out why. There may be a need for deliverance before he is able to put away the sin that so easily besets him. If the problem is a matter of allowing his carnal flesh to rule him, then he must purpose in his heart, "I will not, even though I want to." He must come against his own fleshly drives by an act of his will. When we lay down our wills and allow God to work in our lives, it will show up in our attitudes, words, and actions. More and more we will bear the fruit of His Spirit and not the fruit of our old carnal nature.

After the issue of conversion is settled, the brother's water baptism should be discussed. "Therefore we have been buried with Him through baptism into death, in order that as Christ was raised from the dead through the glory of the Father, so we too might walk in newness of life" (Rom. 6:4). Some churches believe in baptism by the sprinkling of water. However, the word in the Greek which is translated "baptize," is *baptizo* which means, to whelm, that is, to cover wholly with a fluid. Immersion rather than sprinkling is certainly more indicative of the burial spoken of in Romans 6:4 and was the accepted practice in the early church. There is a grace imparted to the believer who obediently follows the Lord into the watery grave of baptism as he demonstrates, more than merely symbolically, the death of the old man, and rises up out of the water into new resurrection life. There is sometimes such an anointing on a new believer that he emerges from the water filled with the Holy Spirit and speaking in tongues.

It is possible that the brother's spiritual life has become weakened by not being nourished with regular communication with God. The new believer, especially, should be encouraged to read the Bible regularly, and to consider the Word of God to be food for his spirit and soul, as vital to his well-being as a balanced diet is to his physical life. "Man shall not live by bread alone, but on every word that proceeds out of the mouth of God" (Matt 4:4). Whatever we read goes into us and becomes part of us whether we remember it or not; it is recorded in the memory banks of the computer we call our brain. The more we feed upon the Word of God, the more we have of His Word within us, vitalizing us, enabling us to respond to the circumstances of life with the mind of Christ. The Lord communicates with us and reveals His will to us through the reading of His word, recalling it to our hearts as we need it.

> How blessed is the man who does not walk in the counsel of the wicked, nor stand in the path of sinners, nor sit in the seat of scoffers! But his delight is in the law of the Lord and in His law he meditates day and night. And he will be like a tree firmly planted by streams of water which yields its fruit in its season, and its leaf does not wither; And in whatever he does, he prospers. (Ps. 1:1-3)

Understanding God's will as expressed in His Word is an important requisite for effective prayer (John 15:7). Prayer is much broader in scope than just being a means of petitioning God for what we want or need, broader, even, than intercession on behalf of another brother or sister. Prayer should be viewed as fellowship with God, through which we offer Him praise, thanksgiving, and adoration (Ps. 141:2). Paul tells us to pray without ceasing (1 Thess. 5:17); that is, to have the perpetual love of Jesus in our hearts so that we are always in an attitude of prayer, ready and willing to pray for anything and everything. As we become increasingly more aware that we live in the presence of God, we may find ourselves awakening with a song in our hearts and praises on our lips, even praying in tongues for hours at a time as we commune with Him (Ps. 91:1-3).

Another potential problem area for the brother in need is the issue of tithing. If he does not see God as his source of provision, if he has not made God the Lord of his finances; the brother will eventually have to repent. A man's heart is where his treasure is (Matt. 6:21).

> "Will a man rob God? Yet you are robbing Me! But you say, 'How have we robbed Thee?' In tithes and contributions. You are cursed with a curse, for you are robbing Me, the whole nation of you! Bring the whole tithe into the storehouse, so that there may be food in My house, and test Me now in this," says the Lord of hosts, "if I will not open for you the windows of heaven, and pour out for you a blessing until there is no more need. Then I will rebuke the devourer for you. . . ." (Mal. 3:8-11)

Ten percent belongs to God as a minimum. Anything else we contribute is an offering of love. We may be tempted to think that we are being generous by giving the control of ten percent to God; but, actually, He is being very generous toward us by letting us keep control of the other ninety percent. If we belong to Him, if we are His slaves, having been purchased by Him at the cost of His blood, then everything we are and everything we have belongs to Him. He, therefore, has the right to command us to return any portion of our income to Him as He so desires. Not to faithfully obey God is to give an advantage to the enemy who can then afflict us because of our disobedience. Our enemy, the devil, stands before God, accusing the saints day and night (Rev. 12:10). If we are guilty on any count, we give an opening to the forces of darkness to take over that area of our life until we repent and surrender it once again to the Lord Jesus (Matt. 18:23-35).

Once when I was ministering in a home meeting, a woman with arthritis came forward for prayer. As she came, the Lord told me the reason for her affliction was that she hated her mother. When it was her turn for prayer, I related to her what the Lord had revealed to me. She burst into tears, admitting it was true; that five years ago her mother had done something which she resented deeply and she had hated her mother from that time. I asked her when she began to suffer from the rheumatoid arthritis and she confessed that it was about the same time as the incident with her mother. Because of her inner condition, the enemy was able to afflict her with a crippling disease. It was necessary for the woman to repent, asking God to forgive her for breaking the fourth commandment—honor thy father and thy mother—and for holding hatred in her heart. She was required to willingly forgive her mother, to make a declaration of love for her, and to promise that the next time they met, she would express that love. We prayed for the woman to be delivered from the grip of spirits of unforgiveness, hate, resentment, and rejection, commanding them to leave her in the name of Jesus. Then we prayed for her to be healed of the arthritis. The woman got up, put down her cane, and walked free from her former pain. Four months later we returned to that area and the woman reported that she had taken a job and had no trace of the arthritis any more. She had gotten rid of all that bitterness and was healed!

The next item to check in our troubled brother's Christian walk is the baptism in the Holy Spirit. If the brother is not walking in victory, if he still lacks the power of the Lord in his life although he is truly a Christian believer, he may need a second touch from God. At first, when Jesus prayed for the blind man in Mark 8:24, his sight was only partially restored, and he reported that he saw men walking as trees. Jesus touched him again and this time the healing was complete. "You shall receive power when the Holy Spirit has come upon you" (Acts 1:8). That promise to the disciples was fulfilled on the day of Pentecost. "And they were all filled with the Holy Spirit and began to speak with other tongues, as the Spirit was giving them utterance" (Acts 2:4). If the brother has had hands laid on him to receive the Holy Spirit and yet has not experienced that power, he should not give up, for the promise is for him as well as all that the Lord calls to himself (Acts 2:39). We can know the joy of being used by the Holy Spirit as His divine life bubbles up out of us. "He who believes in Me, as the Scripture said, 'From his innermost being shall flow rivers of living water.' But this He spoke of the Spirit, whom those who believed in Him were to receive, for the Spirit was not yet given, because Jesus was not yet glorified" (John 7:38-39). This is the baptism of the Holy Spirit which the disciples received, speaking in tongues.

Those who object to speaking in tongues when receiving the Holy Spirit are objecting to a scriptural precedent. It is not our place to tell God that we object to anything He designs. Since the pattern for the first outpouring of the Holy Spirit was that the recipients of that blessing began to speak with other tongues as the Spirit gave them the words, the brother should expect and desire that he, too, will speak with other tongues when the Holy Spirit comes upon him. Speaking in tongues is also called "praying in the Spirit," and is the form of prayer one may use to express the inexpressible yearnings of our subconscious minds, as the Holy Spirit, understanding how we should pray, prays through us (Rom. 8:26). Often there is a limit to our ability to express ourselves when we pray with our understanding. Paul tells us in 1 Corinthians 14:15 that he prays and sings both with the understanding and with the spirit.

A brother's problems often stem not from his vertical relationship with the Lord, but from his horizontal relationships with other people. As he defines his problems: He gets along great with the Lord, but not with his wife or children, or his boss or business associates, or the pastor or fellow-worshippers. His human relationships give him the most trouble and are usually the basis of his need for ministry.

When the brother comes for help, check his home life. Question him on his attitudes and reactions toward those closest to him. It is vital for any believer, particularly for those who wish to minister to others, to have holy relationships at home, for he cannot help but minister from the foundation of those relationships. If he is a rebel, he will foster rebellion in his children; when he ministers to the church, even though he may teach submission, he will pass rebellion on to others. We impart the spirit that motivates us. He might have two faces, the pleasant "churchy" one for the brethren and the snarling beast for the family at home; however, the beast can't remain hidden forever but will be imparted to those being discipled by us. If the brother has a peaceful, joyful wife and happy, submissive children, you can have confidence that he is living up to his responsibilities as the priest of his home. Eph. 5:21-33 and Eph. 6:1-4 teach us how to relate to each other in the home:

> And be subject to one another in the fear of Christ. Wives, be subject to your own husbands as to the Lord. . . . Husbands, love your wives, just as Christ also loved the

> church and gave Himself up for her. . . . Children, obey
> your parents in the Lord, for this is right. . . . Fathers, do
> not provoke your children to anger; but bring them up in
> the discipline and instruction of the Lord.

The only way that this can be effective is if the family members do not use the Word as a club with which to beat each other. Pridefully standing up for our "rights" is the wrong approach and will only cause strife. Strict attention must be given to the scriptural admonitions spoken to oneself, disregarding the others' performance in adhering to the Scriptures addressed to them. As a man honors his wife, laying down his life, his way, his preferences, in deference to her, she will find it easier and easier to submit to him because she can sense his unselfishness. A pleasant, gentle wife who honors her husband as the head of their home, will set the stage for him to give of himself unselfishly to her. There are no guarantees that these responses will be automatic, but we must do our part regardless, for we cannot justify our own disobedience to God because of another's.

The trend in our American culture today, is quite contrary to the model found in the Scriptures. Across our country and increasingly in other lands, many men have resigned from responsible leadership in their homes not only spiritually, but socially as well. As a result, a leadership vacuum has developed and wives have sometimes found it necessary to pick up the burden of directing the life of the family, making final decisions that should be made by the head of the household. In some instances the wife becomes the one who is financially responsible for the upkeep of the home. Authority and responsibility go hand in hand. If a man refuses responsibility for the leadership in his home he will automatically forfeit his authority.

Another contributing factor in the degeneration of the home is the growing confusion between the roles of men and women. This began as the cry of women in the working world for justice—equal pay for equal work; but the women's lib movement, spurred on by lesbian influences, has pushed a just cause into the background and has gone too far by claiming that there are no inherent differences between male and female and that their roles in life can and should be interchangeable. This humanistic understanding is contrary to God's design and will eventually produce perversion.

Many children no longer have godly models of male and female in their homes. Mom is wearing the pants and dad doesn't seem to have an opinion, directing the children to ask their mother for decisions. If dad occasionally does try to lead, mom will overrule him because she "knows" that she will end up having to shoulder the responsibility for the expected resulting mess. Dad is weak and emotional; whereas, mom is a strong disciplinarian who calls the shots by making the plans and setting the policies. Children unconsciously look to their parents for sexual models of what they should grow up to be. Many psychologists believe that the increasing prevalence and openness of homosexuality and lesbianism in the world today is due to the confusion brought about by the reversed roles of father and mother.

The enemy's fervent desire for your family is the destruction of it. He will use any device, however small, to divide and conquer, thereby sterilizing the potent prayers of a united husband and wife who might otherwise overthrow his place in their home and hearts. One has only to recall yesterday's absurd squabble about who ate the last of the ice cream to recognize the reality of this warfare.

> We wrestle not against flesh and blood, but against principalities, against powers, against the rulers of the darkness of this world, against spiritual wickedness in high places. (Eph. 6:2, KJV)

This passage of scripture, interestingly enough, immediately follows the directions for relationships of husbands, wives, children, parents, fathers, employees, and employers. Above all, we must exercise faith in God as we seek to be rightly related to one another. Those problems which cannot and should not be solved by human effort are not beyond hope. God is faithful and no one who ever trusted in Him was ever disappointed. "An arrogant man stirs up strife, but he who trusts in the Lord will prosper" (Prov. 28:25).

In a peaceful, scriptural home, a husband and wife will honor each other, and the husband will extend his blessing to the children as Isaac had a blessing for Jacob and Esau (Gen. 27:7-40), as Jacob (Israel) blessed his sons (Gen. 49:28), and as our heavenly Father blesses us (Eph. 1:3). When I first saw that in the Bible, I began to bless my wife and children. Not only did I ask God to bless them, but I conferred my own blessing upon them and upon my grandchildren.

The brother in need may be ignorant or rebellious concerning God's principles of obedience to church authority (Heb. 13:17) as well as to civil authority (Rom. 13:1-7). It should perhaps be noted here that there is a difference between earthly authority sanctioned by God and anti-Christ tyranny which we must resist as Peter and the apostles did when ordered not to teach any more in the name of Jesus. "But Peter and the apostles answered and said, 'We must obey God rather than men'" (Acts 5:29). Most would agree that we need to obey the laws of the land; if each individual made up his own traffic regulations, there would be heavy carnage on the highways. Obedience to church authority is no less important. If there were no ruling voice to follow in biblical standards of morality and behavior within the church family, the result would be disorder in the meetings and moral decline. Jesus Christ did not come to earth to establish a democracy, but to return us to the law of the Lord (Matt. 5:17-20).

The brother should be instructed that obedience to God is not without great reward.

> "If you will give earnest heed to the voice of the Lord your God, and do what is right in His sight, and give ear to His commandments, and keep all His statutes, I will put none of the diseases on you which I have put on the Egyptians; for I the Lord, am you healer." (Exod. 15:26)

The Lord never suggests; He commands. He has said: heal the sick; raise the dead; cast out demons. As He commands, He empowers us to fulfill His commands. Within the body of Christ we find expression for the ministry to which He has called each of us individually.

And let us consider how to stimulate one another to love and good deeds, not forsaking our own assembling together, as is the habit of some, but encouraging one another, and all the more as you see the day drawing near. (Heb. 10:24-25)

It is important that we be joined together so that we may receive and give life to one another in the context of the family of God.

During my fifteen years in the deliverance ministry, I have seen the emergence of a pattern which indicates that the root cause of most of our problems is rejection. A basic human need is to be loved; one desires to be loved by God, by parents, by husband or wife, by children, and by friends. Even before he is born, a person can suffer the pangs of rejection by a mother who does not want to be pregnant or a father who does not want the added financial burden of another child. There is sometimes so much negative emotion projected from the parents toward the new life, that the child, even as a fetus, becomes bound by an evil spirit. A child who enters the world in this condition will be troubled for years until the Lord sets him free, not knowing why he feels rejected by his family, teachers, and friends, although his parents may have since accepted and loved him. His whole personality may have been built upon the understanding that no one really loves and cares for him. In ministering to the brother who has a problem of rejection, we should determine the origin of his problem, and after dispelling the evil spirit, pray that these inner wounds would be healed.

Rejection often produces rebellion. The unloved, unwanted child will often conclude that he has to make his own way and seek his own best interests, initially rejecting parental authority and then other authority, including God's. We are living in an age of rebellion when many young people are doing their own thing, rejecting the religious beliefs and standards of their parents. The breakdown of the home in our culture has attendant with it increased promiscuity and a soaring crime rate.

The entertainment media portrays blatantly the depth of immorality to which our generation has descended. Indeed, now, a new morality has emerged, one where free sex is "honest" and "beautiful." Divorce is the quick and easy way to get rid of a tiresome relationship. Abortion is commonly sought to end the problem of an "inconvenient" pregnancy. Getting high on drugs or alcohol is "having fun." Homosexuality is the expression of an acceptable alternate "sexual preference." Stealing is "okay" as long as you don't get caught, and occult practices are a respectable way for people to be "helped." Those who have been formed in the mold of such a value system will most certainly feel its imprint upon their souls. Many, if not most of the heroes in today's dramas, are brutal, promiscuous and foulmouthed, not at all like the man in the white hat, riding the white horse—our hero of days gone by.

There has appeared a line of demarcation between the old-fashioned Christian standards, which even non-Christians accepted just a few decades ago. This new morality of humanism has no absolute values and no law of God to govern it. We are alarmed to note that this departure from the standard of God's laws has begun to infiltrate the churches in much the same way that Israel departed from the true God and went after false gods at various times in her history. A person or people who departs from God's standards, and does not repent, will be judged severely by God. The brother who has been schooled in the lusts of this perverse generation in which we live, giving himself unknowingly but willingly into the hands of demonic powers who now hold him in bondage, even after repenting and dedicating himself to the Lord, may have constant warfare within himself, until he expels these spirits from his life.

If the brother confesses that he often finds himself feeling, doing, and saying things that he doesn't want to, things which violate his conscience, then the minister should instruct him from the Word how to put off the deeds of the flesh and assist him through deliverance wherever necessary. The brother may deceive himself into believing that his problem is not serious because he is only a "little" resentful, or a "little" angry; but a "little" bondage is still a bondage, a "little" demon is still a demon, and could grow up into a "big" one if allowed to remain, festering and infecting the brother's life more extensively.

When a man speaks, he reveals what is in his heart (Matt. 12:34). For example, if the brother frequently jokes in an off-color way, or if he speaks often about his fears, or expresses hatred for someone, he is revealing something about his inner condition. If he resists or postpones dealing with these inner problems, he should be warned that to do so may be dangerous.

> But each one is tempted when he is carried away and enticed by his own lust. Then when lust has conceived, it gives birth to sin; and when sin is accomplished, it brings forth death. Therefore putting aside all filthiness and all that remains of wickedness, in humility receive the word implanted, which is able to save your souls. (James 1:14, 15, 21)

Allowing hidden sins to remain or allowing strong persistent temptations to bombard the mind, can result in demon bondage, and may be an indication that demon bondage is already established. The brother should be made aware that God will not hear him if he holds onto evil ways (Ps. 66:18). The enemy will, if the brother is unrepentant, gradually lead him deeper and deeper into sin. All of us have heard via the news media of someone who murdered for no apparent reason, driven to do so by some inner force or voice, which he even identifies as "god." The seeds of destruction can grow from rejection to rebellion, resentment, hatred, and then, finally even to murder. For the Christian, this is unthinkable. Yet, look at the story of evangelist Jim Jones of Guyana infamy. "Small" issues of attitude and temptation grew hidden in his heart until they developed into open sin, and finally erupted into perversion, mass murder, and suicide, all in the name of "God."

Jesus came to give us an abundant, blessed life. He said, "The thief comes only to steal, and kill, and destroy; I came that they might have life, and might have it abundantly" (John 10:10). We must be persuaded to confess our sins and repent from them or we will not be able to walk in the overcoming victory that earmarks an abundant life.

One time, a sister called me on the phone at 3:00 A.M. She said that there was an unholy presence in her room and she could hear voices laughing at her. I instructed her to tell them to get out of her room in the name of Jesus. She answered that she had attempted to do that, but they wouldn't leave. I prayed for a word from the Lord and He showed me a deep, dark pool of water. When I asked Him what it was, He told me it was the sin of abortion. I asked the sister, "Did you ever have an abortion?" She replied that she did and that she had never confessed it. I told her that it was her deep dark secret, symbolized by the pool in my vision, and directed her to confess it to the Lord and ask Him for forgiveness. She immediately did. Then, I told those tormenting demons to leave her house in Jesus' name and they left.

I am amazed to find that many women do not realize that when they have an abortion, they are actually committing murder. They tuck that incident away into the past and forget about it, not connecting it with their present distress until the Lord reveals it to them. Just as the sister was directed to repent of the sin, to confess it to the Lord, and to ask for forgiveness, so must one do with any other sin, no matter how long ago it was committed.

David illustrates graphically to us the consequences of un-confessed sin.

> How blessed is he whose transgression is forgiven, whose sin is covered! How blessed is the man to whom the Lord does not impute iniquity, and in whose spirit there is no deceit! When I kept silent about my sin, my body wasted away through my groaning all day long. For day and night Thy hand was heavy upon me; My vitality was drained away as with the fever-heat of summer. I acknowledged my sin to Thee, and my iniquity I did not hide; I said, "I will confess my transgressions to the Lord"; and Thou didst forgive the guilt of my sin. Therefore, let everyone who is godly pray to Thee in a time when Thou mayest be found. (Ps. 32:1-6)

We see from this passage, that unconfessed sin can result in physical and emotional suffering and that repentance and confession will bring forgiveness and relief.

There has never before been such a widespread, popular involvement with occultism as in this present day. Everybody seems to know the sign of the zodiac under which they were born, even if they don't read their daily horoscope. The brother in need may think such things as Ouija boards, tarot cards, fortunetelling, transcendental meditation, are merely innocent games or pasttimes. not realizing that they come under the same heading of "occult" as witchcraft, the consulting of mediums, devil worship and soul projection.

> The Spirit explicitly says that in later times some will fall away from the faith, paying attention to deceitful spirits and doctrines of demons, by means of the hypocrisy of liars seared in their own conscience as with a branding iron. (1 Tim. 4:1, 2)

If, at any time, the brother has dabbled in the occult, he has violated the first commandment of God which says, "You shall have no other gods before Me. You shall not worship them or serve them; for I, the Lord your God, am a jealous God, visiting the iniquity of the fathers on the children, on the third and fourth generations of those who hate Me" (Exod. 20:2, 5). In diagnosing the brother's problem, the minister may learn that the involvement with occultism may be through the brother's parents, or grandparents, or even through his great-grandparents, four generations ago.

Just as a person can inherit a physical infirmity or defect, so can a spiritual disability be passed down, as the Scripture says, on to the third or fourth generations. These influences, standards, and customs can be passed from parent to child. I have seen this time and time again. When people are led through the prayer to renounce the source of affliction and bondage that has come down through the generations, they are set free. The brother must rid his home of all occult books, ornaments, and influences after he has determined to turn away from such evil.

God desires that we would hate what He hates, and more than anything else, He hates spiritual adultery; which is what happens when a person turns away from Him and turns to other gods. When a person commits spiritual adultery, he denies God and consults evil spirits for guidance, for information, for comfort, and for kicks. "Hate evil, you who love the Lord, who preserves the souls of His godly ones; He delivers them from the hand of the wicked" (Ps. 97:10). Those who are allied with God will say with David, "Do I not hate those who hate Thee, O Lord? And do I not loathe those who rise up against Thee? I hate them with the utmost hatred; they have become my enemies'' (Ps. 139:21, 22).

Every minister of deliverance should keep uppermost in his mind and heart that Jesus is his Lord and that he extends Jesus' ministry to those in need. Our purpose is to serve, to wash the dirt of the world off the feet of our brothers and sisters in the same way that Jesus humbly washed the feet of the disciples at the Last Supper (John 13:5-17). It was customary in those days when people entered a home, for a slave to wash the feet of the master and his guests. At this Passover gathering, however, no slave appeared, and Jesus took it upon himself to lay His garments aside, ''and taking a towel, girded himself about. Then He poured water into the basin and began to wash the disciples' feet, and to wipe them with the towel with which He was girded (John 13:4, 5). Peter was indignant and embarrassed by the position to which Jesus had lowered himself, especially since he knew himself to be lower than Jesus. Peter tried to refuse the Lord from serving him in this way; but Jesus said, ''You call me Teacher and Lord; and you are right; for so I am. If I then, the Lord and the Teacher, washed your feet, you also ought to wash one another's feet. For I gave you an example that you also should do as I did to you. Truly, truly, I say to you, a slave is not greater than his master; neither one who is sent greater than the one who sent him. If you know these things, you are blessed if you do them'' (John 13:13-17). If we desire to minister, then we must be willing to be a lowly servant. Sometimes this means we have to do the things we don't want to do, meeting the needs of unlovely people, spending time with them, caring for them, washing their feet.

One day as I was busily running errands, I saw a woman I knew lying on the street in the throes of an epileptic seizure, with a policeman by her side. I was tired and very much tempted to hurry on by and let the policeman handle the situation. The Lord reminded me that this was His child, my sister, and that I should serve her with His love. So, I went to the policeman, told him that I was a minister, that I knew the woman and that I would take care of her. I left the sister at her doctor's office and later on he called me to come and pick her up and take her home. I confess that even though I was obedient to the Lord, it was not what I preferred to do; but the servant of the Lord must turn his will over to the Lord and do as he is bidden.

God is faithful to refresh and strengthen us in our laborings for His name's sake. We will be blessed as we fellowship with Him as His life and His ministry flow through us. As His followers we are sent to perform, not only the things He did, but even "greater works than these . . ." (John 14:12).

We like to be on top of every situation—God's man of faith and power—able to heal with a touch, deliver with a word, see people fall to the ground under the power of God as we lay our hands upon them, able to leap tall buildings with a single bound like some kind of super-saint. However, Jesus instructs that, "those who are recognized as rulers of the Gentiles lord it over them; and their great men exercise authority over them. But it is not so among you, but whoever wishes to become great among you shall be your servant; and whoever wishes to be first among you shall be slave of all. For even the Son of Man did not come to be served, but to serve and to give His life a ransom for many (Mark 10:42-45).

Jesus who has been called the Great Physician, was, and still is, precise in His diagnosis of and ministry to the needs of His followers. He applied the appropriate remedy to each need, laying down His position as Creator and becoming the suffering servant. Considering ourselves as servants should not weaken us; rather, it should strengthen us, recognizing that we have a holy mission and that our calling and purpose is to bring glory and honor to the name above all names, Jesus, the anointed Son of the living God.

TWO
DISCERNING
OF SPIRITS

In Paul's first letter to the Corinthian church, he instructed them on spiritual gifts, explaining that he wanted them to be informed about these matters. He is careful to note that the believer may have different gifts but it is the same Holy Spirit who gives them; that there are different ways of serving God, but it is the same Lord Jesus who is served; that God works through different people in different ways, but it is still the same God who achieves His purposes through them all (1 Cor. 12:1-7).

In this chapter we will discuss the characteristics of the manifestations of the Holy Spirit, differentiating them from the manifestations of evil spirits and from that part of man's nature which is his own human spirit. Paul desired that we would have insight into spiritual matters so that we could sort out truth from error and deception. Although we are assailed by Satan before we are saved and baptized in the Holy Spirit, we are even more so attacked afterwards, entering more actively into spiritual warfare: we, as temples of the Holy Spirit, are now prepared to storm the gates of hell which cannot prevail against us, while the enemy seeks to overthrow this now powerful stronghold of the Lord in our lives.

As we become increasingly aware of this conflict between the forces of darkness and of light, especially after being baptized in the Holy Spirit, we find that we need to be able to discern which of three voices is communicating with us: the voice of the Lord, the Holy Spirit; the unholy spirit and any one of his demonic cohorts; and our own human spirit. All of these speak to us through the channel of our minds, and until we learn to discern the different character of each, it can be very confusing to determine which voice we are actually hearing.

We should realize that it would be easy to think we have spiritual discernment when all we really have is suspicion. Suspicion is based upon what we have learned about an individual or situation, from either our personal knowledge or from the accuser who whispers lies to us, rather than upon knowledge which comes strictly from the Holy Spirit. Unfortunately, many charismatics operate in the "gift" of suspicion and cause much dissension and division within the church. The devil is a great deceiver, coming often as an angel of light, who tries to deceive the saints. If he can keep us fighting among ourselves, we will be too busy to do battle against him.

Not only must we judge the thoughts and impulses which enter our minds, but also the words which are spoken as prophecy from the Lord. Rarely will one find in the Christian church a false prophet speaking under the influence of a demonic power; more often we see a mixture of Holy Spirit and of human motivated prophecies.

> "I have heard what the prophets have said who prophesy falsely in My name, saying, 'I had a dream, I had a dream!' How long? Is there anything in the hearts of the prophets who prophesy falsehood, even these prophets of the deception of their own heart." (Jer. 23:25-26)

That is why Paul says that all prophecy must be judged. "And let two or three prophets speak, and let the others pass judgment" (1 Cor. 14:29). The necessity of evaluating prophecy is also true for the fledgling prophet. When he or she first speaks a prophetic word, there will most likely be more of the prophet than the Lord in the words. "For we know in part, and we prophesy in part" (1 Cor. 13:10). This should change as the prophet matures in his gift and learns to hear the Lord more clearly. Then the balance will be in the other direction: more of the Lord and less of the prophet.

A young man came to me once and said that the Lord had told him something which was very private and had instructed him not to check it out with anyone. This immediately alerted me because of John's direction:

> Beloved, do not believe every spirit, but test the spirits to see whether they are from God; because many false prophets have gone out into the world. (1 John 4:1)

As a further admonition, Paul tells the Corinthians that every fact is to be confirmed by the testimony of two or three witnesses (2 Cor. 13:1). The young man refused to share the word he had received. As time went on, he showed evidence of being unteachable and rebellious. As of this writing, he is fallen away from the faith.

We need to be informed in order to be armed against the wiles and snares of the devil who would do anything to get us back into his camp as we were before we gave ourselves to Jesus. Ignorance of the enemy is the reason that many Christians are afflicted and wounded by all sorts of demonically caused problems, physically, intellectually, emotionally and spiritually. "My people are destroyed for lack of knowledge," says the Lord (Hosea 4:6). With that in mind, let us go through the Scriptures and examine the capabilities of demons.

1. *They have knowledge.* "And just then there was in their synagogue a man with an unclean spirit; and he cried out, saying, 'What do we have to do with You, Jesus of Nazareth? Have You come to destroy us? I know who You are—the Holy One of God!'" (Mark 1:23-24).
2. *They have the power of speech through the person they inhabit.* (Mark 1:24).
3. *They express their desires.* "And the demons began to entreat Him, saying, 'If You are going to cast us out, send us into the herd of swine'" (Matt. 8:31).
4. *They fear.* "And they were entreating Him not to command them to depart into the abyss" (Luke 8:31).
5. *They have need of rest.* "Now when the unclean spirit goes out of a man, it passes through waterless places,

seeking rest, and does not find it" (Matt. 12:43).

6. *They have a will and can make decisions.* "Then it says, 'I will return to my house from which I came'... Then it goes, and takes along with it seven other spirits more wicked than itself, and they go in and live there; and the last state of that man becomes worse than the first. This is the way it will also be with this evil generation" (Matt. 12:44, 45).

7. *They can be exceedingly fierce.* "...two men who were demon-possessed met Him as they were coming out of the tombs; they were so exceedingly violent that no one could pass by that road" (Matt. 8:28).

8. *They have great strength.* "But there were some itinerant Jewish exorcists who attempted to invoke the name of the Lord Jesus when dealing with those who had evil spirits. They would say, 'I command you in the name of Jesus whom Paul preaches.' Seven brothers, sons of a chief priest called Sceva, were engaged in this practice on one occasion, when the evil spirit answered, "Jesus I know, and I know about Paul, but who are you? And the man in whom the evil spirit was living sprang at them and overpowered them all with such violence that they rushed out of that house wounded, with their clothes torn off their backs" (Acts 19:13-16, Phillips New Testament).

9. *They can possess animals as well as humans.* "And the demons came out from the man and entered the swine; and the herd rushed down the steep bank into the lake, and were drowned" (Luke 8:33).

10. *They have the power to foretell.* "And it happened that as we were going to the place of prayer, a certain slave-girl having a spirit of divination met us, who was bringing her masters much profit by fortune-telling" (Acts 16:16).

During a deliverance session, the minister should be cautious when demons give out any information as they are not of God and quite often will lie. Instead, he must depend upon the Holy Spirit who will give true discernment and whatever knowledge and wisdom that is needed.

11. *They can counterfeit the works of God.* The magicians of Egypt were able to turn their staffs into serpents just as the Lord did with Aaron's staff; but Aaron's serpent swallowed up theirs (Exod. 7:9-12). God will have the ultimate victory!

One may ask, how can the devil heal or do any other apparently good thing and why would he? Satan is a fallen angel who still retains all the power he had when he belonged to God. Only now, he uses his power to deceive and lead people away from the Lord, to get them to serve him and, ultimately, to destroy them. At the very least, his aim is to confuse the saints of God, rendering them helpless and useless, and to bring dishonor to the name of Jesus.

It is fairly easy to recognize the works of darkness in the world around us: pornography, murder, violence, child abuse and occultism; and we know that the devil has made many gains. However, it is not so easy to recognize the work of the enemy within the church. That is why Paul instructs the Galatians to live by the Spirit of God and to crucify the flesh with its passions and desires. He lists these works of the flesh so that the Galatians would recognize where they were falling short: "immorality, impurity, sensuality, idolatry, sorcery, enmities, strife, jealousy, outbursts of anger, disputes, dissensions, factions, envyings, drunkenness, carousings and things like these, of which I forewarn you just as I have forewarned you that those who practice such things shall not inherit the kingdom of God" (Gal. 5:19-21). Paul contrasts the works of the flesh with the fruit of the Holy Spirit. For further clarity, let us note that anything that is opposed to that fruit, is not of God's Spirit and well might be listed with the deeds of the flesh, where Paul says, "and things like these."

The fruit of the Spirit	*The Antithesis*
1. Love	1. hate, rejection, hostility
2. Joy	2. vexation, depression, despair
3. Peace	3. contention, disorder, discord, worry, quarreling, insecurity, fearfulness

4. Patience	4. impatience, restlessness, intolerance
5. Kindness	5. cruelty, harshness, inconsideration
6. Goodness	6. malice, evil, depravity, perversion, stinginess, threatenings
7. Faithfulness	7. disloyalty, dishonesty, adultery, unreliability, fickleness
8. Gentleness	8. stubbornness, hardness, egotism, impoliteness, violence, severity
9. Self-control	9. lack of restraint, rebellion, instability

When a man has entrenched within his heart, motives, attitudes, and actions which are contrary to the Spirit of God, he may need deliverance, as well as repentance, from spirits which have the same name as his sins.

Jesus instructed His followers to pray and minister in His name. It is not enough for one to pray in the name of "God" for there are many gods in this world. "Every spirit that does not confess Jesus is not from God; and this is the spirit of antichrist of which you have heard that it is coming, and now it is already in the world" (1 John 4:3). So, be specific about the name of Jesus as you minister and encourage others to do likewise.

> "In My name they will cast out demons, they will speak with new tongues; they will pick up serpents, and if they drink any deadly poison, it shall not hurt them; they will lay hands on the sick, and they will recover." (Mark 16:17, 18)

A woman came to our home recently who had had twelve accidents in the last five years. During one of these accidents, just after her car had slammed into a telephone pole, she saw a bright light and an image which spoke to her and identified himself as God. The apparition directed her to get a crucifix and wear it always and that it would be protection for her. She got a crucifix for herself and one for her husband, but she continued to have accidents, nearly getting killed each time.

The voice spoke to her again telling her, "I am God. I will

give you great power, if, when you pray for people, you will say three times, 'in the name of God'." She began to do this and people were being healed. I told her that she was in error according to Scripture. (Remember that Pharoah's magicians could work miracles, too.) First of all, she was using the crucifix as an amulet or charm for protection instead of relying upon the Lord Jesus himself as He promises to protect us in His word (Ps. 91). Secondly, Jesus directs us:

> "And whatever you ask in My name, that will I do, that the Father may be glorified in the Son. If you ask Me anything in My name, I will do it." (John 14:13, 14)

This was not the only time I ministered to a person who used a religious ornament as protection against evil. (Those who do this are under the deception that this is a righteous means of protection.) I once went to a man's home to pray for his healing. He had an unbelievably large collection of religious statues in the various rooms of his house—a shrine in each room. Also, around his neck he had a crucifix and other religious medals which were supposed to protect him from all kinds of problems. This man was so fearful, he would not leave his house, except on rare occasions. I asked him, if he was so protected by wearing all those medals, why was he still afraid to leave his house. I said to him, "Look at me. What do I wear?" He answered, "Well, I don't see anything." Then I told him that my protection is within me. I have the Holy Spirit, and because I do, I know that the Lord Jesus Christ protects me by His blood.

I instructed him to get rid of all his religious ornaments and statues which he had used as charms against evil, but he refused. Several months later he called me and told me that the Lord had convicted him of his idolatry. He, his wife, and their children had gone through their home and had broken every one of those statues. At first the children had been afraid to destroy them, but after breaking the first ones, they realized that there was no power in them and they willingly smashed them all. That brother is healed today since he learned that safety and healing come to him through the name and the blood of Jesus. There is no other way.

Jesus said of himself:

> "I am the way, the truth, and the life" (John 14:6). "I am the door; if anyone enters through Me, he shall be saved" (John 10:9). "He who does not enter by the door into the fold of the sheep, but climbs up some other way, he is a thief and a robber" (John 10:1).

This is true not only for salvation and healing, but for all the gifts of the Holy Spirit. It is the Holy Spirit who bears witness to our hearts that Jesus is Lord. If we go any other way, we are choosing a way that God did not designate. As we mentioned earlier, the devil can counterfeit the manifestations of the Holy Spirit; however, Satan is a thief who comes only to steal, kill and destroy (John 10:10).

At a Catholic charismatic retreat, a large group of us were gathered together praising the Lord when a woman near us began to speak in tongues. Both the priest and I felt uneasy about her utterance, so I called her aside to discuss it with her. I asked her how she had received her gift of tongues and she said, "At home, while I was praying, it came to me." After explaining 1 John 4:1 to the woman, she agreed to put her gift of tongues to the test. I commanded the spirit by which she spoke to be bound and powerless in the name of Jesus. Then I led her to praise the Lord with me again in tongues, but she couldn't any more.

Now, I can tell the Holy Spirit to be bound in the name of Jesus, but I know that it won't work because the Holy Spirit is God. I can, however, bind any other spirit in the name of Jesus, and I know it will work because the name of Jesus is greater than any of them. Then I asked the sister if she was into horoscopes, Santeria, and other occult practices. She admitted that she was.

I invited her to come the next day to my home at which time my wife and I delivered her from many evil spirits. We led the woman through salvation and the baptism of the Holy Spirit; and this time, when she prayed in tongues, it was altogether different from the day before. She was really blessed by God and today is a vital force in the Spanish-speaking charismatic movement in South Florida. Like this sister, others who have sought guidance through witchcraft, Santeria, spiritualism and other occult means will need deliverance and may have to reexamine their whole spiritual foundation, perhaps even going back through the elementary steps of salvation to the cross of Jesus.

The religion, Santeria, came with the Lucumi tribes from Africa when they were brought to the Caribbean as slaves. They believe in multitudes of gods and goddesses and have one for every need. Their religion became mixed together with the Catholic religion of the slaveholders (without the Catholic Church's sanction). For over 500 years this religion was passed on until today is seen in the Caribbean as a confusing combination of the two.

In Genesis 3, when Satan came to Adam and Eve, he offered them something that was apparently good; the ability to distinguish between good and evil so that they would be like God. However, the Lord had commanded them not to eat of the tree of knowledge of good and evil, but had offered them the fruit of the tree of life, which was God's gift of himself. The prerogative of determining what is good and what is evil belongs to the Creator alone and to no other. When they disobeyed they were no longer entitled to receive life from the Lord for they had chosen the forbidden fruit of independent decision and judgment and self-determination.

We face the same choice today: God's way versus ours; God's commands versus our good ideas. When entering the spiritual realm, we must enter through the narrow gate, Jesus. God says that He is a jealous God and we must not have any false gods before Him. If a person goes to a medium or psychic healer, he is going through that medium to the devil. When that happens, he enters the kingdom of darkness and opens himself up for the demonic powers to indwell him. He may receive a temporary healing and feel good for a little while, but eventually will suffer great loss, and bit by bit, perhaps even suffer the loss of his soul. The minister of deliverance will find that much physical and mental illness, including depression, cancer, arthritis and suicidal tendencies, is due to a person's past involvement with the occult. The remedy for this is repentance and deliverance in the name of Jesus; for His blood was shed to cleanse us from all sin and all forms of unrighteousness. "If we walk in the light as He Himself is in the light, we have fellowship with one another, and the blood of Jesus His Son cleanses us from all sin,"

(1 John 1:7), just as the blood of the lamb protected the Israelites from the angel of death (Exod. 12:13).

How often have we sung the words, "There is power, power, wonder-working power, in the blood of the Lamb," without realizing the extent of the power that there is in His blood. Without the shedding of blood there is no forgiveness of sin (Heb. 9:22). It was through Jesus' shed blood on Calvary that we were redeemed from the hands of Satan (Eph. 1:7); and through the shed blood of Jesus, the Lamb of God, Satan's kingdom is overthrown (Rev. 12:11). It is by the blood of Jesus that we may enter into the holy presence of the Lord (Heb. 10:19); and it is by the blood of Jesus that we are sanctified (Heb. 13:12). It isn't any wonder that the devil and his friends do not want to hear about the blood of Jesus. There are times when ministering in the name of Jesus, especially when there is a great deal mentioned about His shed blood, that demonic powers are stirred up visibly and vocally during a meeting, sometimes screaming or challenging much to everyone's surprise. It is the nature of these powers to disrupt in this manner in order to call attention away from the Lord. They cannot stand to hear songs or teachings about the blood of Jesus.

Once during such a meeting, while we were praising the Lord, a young woman slipped down in her seat. A few people around her remarked that she had been "slain in the Spirit." When anyone falls down under the power of God, I want to know the reason for it. Sometimes it is because God is healing or blessing them, but sometimes it is because they are in rebellion and resisting God. For example, when the guards came to seize Jesus in the garden, they all fell to the ground as He spoke to them (John 18:6). Sometimes, however, a person will fall to the floor because he is being torn by demonic forces within him as he experiences the presence of God. "And they brought the boy to Him. And when he saw Him, immediately the spirit threw him into a convulsion, and falling to the ground, he began rolling about and foaming at the mouth" (Mark 9:20).

The Lord showed me that this sister was in need of deliverance. I went over to her and whispered in her ear, "Don't you dare interfere, you demons, until this meeting is over." Then addressing the girl, "Now, get up and sit down." The meeting went on with prayer and a sermon; but as soon as it was all over, down she went again. After we dismissed the others, my wife and I and the girl's husband prayed for a couple of hours. We learend that this girl was having a love affair with a demon called Incubus. Webster's dictionary defines incubus as an evil spirit who tries to lie on sleeping persons, especially women, with whom it seeks sexual intercourse. The girl had never been able to have intercourse with her husband in the three years of their marriage because she was too small, even though she had had surgery in an attempt to correct the problem. She was getting comfort from this demon and had come to love it, not realizing that he had afflicted her with this condition so that he could have her for himself. After she finally renounced it, we were able to command it to come out of her in the name of Jesus. Then we prayed for her to be healed of her physical impairment. As we prayed, she reported that she felt a stretching sensation. A week later, the couple returned and happily told us that for the first time, they had had normal marital relations. She was healed. Praise the Lord!

A minister of deliverance is not exempt from needing deliverance himself. The enemy can entice a man through pride to follow a false path that the Lord has not chosen. "You are a specially chosen messenger of God." "You are more advanced than others." "You have a higher calling than other Christians." "You must give up your occupation and live by faith." "You should leave your wife and children because they do not complement your ministry." Some are led down a path of frustration and unfruitfulness because of listening to voices or leadings like these, losing their homes and their credibility as Christians, and leading others astray after them. If a man is led by his impulses, emotions, goose bumps, apparitions, or words which appeal to his pride and vanity, he may find himself one day being led about by a familiar spirit which is masquerading as God. There is safety in a multitude of counselors (Prov. 24:6) and a wise man will seek confirmation from his brothers before accepting any revelation or directive as the word of God for him. Although there are occasions when the Lord wants us to bypass our natural reasoning and trust Him in a particular situation, He doesn't want us to throw out discernment or good common sense." 'Come now, and let us reason together,' says the Lord" (Isa. 1:18). God created us in His image, having a will, intellect, and memory. He desires that we would love and serve Him with our whole being, which does not negate any spiritual gift He might give to us. The enemy, on the other hand, clamors confusingly and persistently, urging sudden action without allowing us time to reason or intelligently weigh the issues.

Some people with familiar spirits have admitted that they are aware that the voice they hear is not God's voice, but they argue that it is the voice of their guardian angel. It is true that there are guardian angels. "For He will give His angels charge concerning you, to guard you in all your ways. They will bear you up in their hands, lest you strike your foot against a stone" (Ps. 91:11, 12); but it is also true that enemy spirits try to guide us in order to lead us into destruction.

The cartoon we have seen of the man with an angel on one shoulder and a demon on the other shoulder, both trying to influence him, accurately illustrates this. If the man turns away from the voice of the angel of the Lord long enough and follows the voice of the demon, he will be snared, a slave of that spirit. "Do you not know that when you present yourselves to someone as slaves for obedience, you are slaves of the one whom you obey, either of sin resulting in death, or of obedience resulting in righteousness?" (Rom. 6:16).

Although we can effectively deal with demonic powers by casting them out in the name of Jesus, let us not forget that the only way to deal with the carnal nature of man is the way of the cross: crucifixion—that is, self-denial, and self-control, putting to death the works and impulses of the flesh. "I have been crucified with Christ; and it is no longer I who live, but Christ lives in me; and the life which I now live in the flesh I live by faith in the Son of God, who loved me and delivered Himself up for me" (Gal. 2:20).

If the believer can truly make this claim, the evidence will be that he no longer considers that he has any rights, neither has he any other will besides the will of the Lord, nor has he any desire to sin. He is crucified and dead! With David, our prayer must be:

> Create in me a clean heart, O God, and renew a steadfast spirit within me. Do not cast me away from Thy presence, and do not take Thy Holy Spirit from me. Restore to me the joy of Thy salvation, and sustain me with a willing

spirit. Then I will teach transgressors Thy ways, and sinners will be converted to Thee. (Ps. 51:10-13)

I strongly suggest that one who feels called to minister in deliverance first undergo deliverance himself. He should spend some time learning from those who have proven their ministry in this area in order to be prepared to deal with any situation, however bizarre.

When my wife Evelyn and I were first baptized in the Holy Spirit and trying to minister to a friend with a spirit of stubbornness, we knew very little about what we were doing. After working for a while against the stubborn spirit, Evelyn had an idea. She said to me, "I'll take that spirit into me, and then you can cast it out of me." No sooner had she said that, when an evil spirit entered into her. When I spoke to her, she snapped back, "Don't you talk to me that way!" and I knew that stubborn spirit was in her. I said, "Oh, my goodness" and tried to cast it out. She turned and walked away from me refusing to have me minister to her. Evelyn got on her hands and knees and crawled under the piano and so did I, following her and trying to deliver her by laying the Bible upon her back. I really didn't know what I was doing. This was certainly not the result we had anticipated when we began to pray for our friend.

Instead of just our friend having a spirit of stubbornness, now both the friend and my wife had one. We needed some help! At that point, my daughter phoned and I asked her to pray. Then, I called on the Lord and I commanded that spirit to leave Evelyn and it did. Believe me, we didn't make the same mistake again. It seems humorous now, looking back on that incident, but others have tried to take on another's demons, and the end of the story was not so funny. In the newspaper, just the other day, I read about a young man who called the demons out of his young friend into himself. They caused him to commit murder and his little friend was left in the same bound condition that he had been in at the start. One should never try to minister outside of the protection of other members of the body of Christ. When Jesus appointed seventy to minister in His name, He sent them out two by two (Luke 10:1-20). No man alone has the mind of Christ but we do have it corporately (1 Cor. 2:16).

When ministering deliverance to a brother in need, the

minister usually needs to know the name of the spirit. The brother must willingly renounce the demon and repent, that is, turn away from, the effects, attitudes, and actions committed while under the influence of that evil bondage. If there is need for more than one demon to be cast out, it is important to determine the name of the strong ruling one because it makes a place in the brother for other related spirits to enter. For example, if the ruling spirit is suicide, then its companion spirits might be; self-pity, grief, despair, rejection, loneliness and escapism. Usually, that strong one will evade recognition. It has great authority in the brother's life and will continue to harass and drive him, even though the brother may seek deliverance time and time again, casting out the same lesser, more easily discerned spirits each time until the strong ruling spirit is discerned and expelled. "But if I cast out demons by the Spirit of God, then the kingdom of God has come upon you. Or how can anyone enter the strong man's house and carry off his property, unless he first binds the strong man? And then he will plunder his house" (Matt. 12:28, 29).

When someone comes to us for deliverance, usually we follow a certain format. Before we begin, we always worship the Lord and ask Him for a word of knowledge, a word of wisdom, and discerning of spirits and we believe that God will grant just that. We trust Him to illume our minds with whatever we need to be able to minister. Of course, a person can present himself for deliverance and not receive it. He must cooperate with those who are ministering to him, and be willing to expose his inner self, renounce all the works and pomps of Satan, and give himself totally to the Lord Jesus Christ. The brother will not accomplish much if he holds onto a favorite demon, not wanting to give up a pet sin; but if he is willing and obedient, God will hear his cry and he will be set free. "A broken and a contrite heart, O God, Thou wilt not despise" (Ps. 51:17).

Many evil spirits will leave a new believer when he receives the Holy Spirit, but others will remain until they are rejected and cast out. Often, they will remain hidden and if the brother considers seeking deliverance, the spirits will convince him that he doesn't need it, or that he doesn't want it. A young man came to see me one time for counseling and in the middle of our session, a demon identified himself as "Lucky." The man explained that he smoked Lucky Strike cigarettes. When I asked him if he was willing to give up smoking, he replied that he wasn't willing because he enjoyed smoking.

I stopped the deliverance session right at that point, much to the brother's dismay, explaining to him that as long as he holds on to a demon, it will become a bridge across which all the other demons from which he had just been delivered can re-enter him. He pleaded with me to continue as there were things in his life he wanted very much to get rid of, but since he was still unwilling to give up smoking, "Lucky" remained and I could not continue.

On another occasion, we returned from a prayer meeting late one night and two people came to our house with a woman who was intoxicated. I discerned that she had some sort of occult spirit. When I asked the woman to name the spirit, she told me that it was the spirit of Agnes, a dear friend who had died in her arms. She said that she loved Agnes and wanted to keep her. I explained to the woman that when Agnes died, she went to be with the Lord and that this was an evil spirit who was pretending to be Agnes. When I told her that although she loved Agnes, she should hate this lying spirit who had deceived her, the woman refused. I told the woman and her companions that I couldn't help if the woman wouldn't cooperate. They argued with me and then declared that they would go elsewhere to find help. I replied that they could try, but any true minister of Jesus Christ would tell them the same thing I had.

Disappointing and heartbreaking as it can be, even when the minister knows the solution to a problem, there are times when the one in need is the very one blocking the help. Jesus understood this when He lamented, "O Jerusalem, Jerusalem, who kills the prophets and stones those who are sent to her! How often I wanted to gather your children together, the way a hen gathers her chicks under her wings, and you were unwilling. Behold, your house is being left to you desolate" (Matt. 23:37, 38).

God has provided everything for us that we need to defeat the enemy; first of all, we defeat the devil by the blood of the Lamb (Rev. 12:11). God has given to the church the gifts of the Holy Spirit, including discerning of spirits, to enable the believer to recognize the work of the enemy. Also, He has given us the full armor of God as our protection to enable us to stand firm against the schemes of the devil (Eph. 6:11).

> Therefore, take up the full armor of God, that you may be able to resist in the evil day, and having done everything, to stand firm. Stand firm therefore, having girded your loins with truth, and having put on the breastplate of righteousness, and having shod your feet with the preparation of the gospel of peace; in addition to all, taking up the shield of faith with which you will be able to extinguish all the flaming missiles of the evil one. And take the helmet of salvation, and the sword of the Spirit which is the word of God. (Eph. 6:13-17)

Notice that all of the elements listed in the previous Scripture are of a defensive nature with the exception of the sword of the Spirit which is the Word of God. That Word was embodied in the person of Jesus Christ and is the only offensive weapon we will ever need against the enemy. We need to know the written word of God and be able to speak it confidently in our warfare just as Jesus did when he was tested in the desert after forty days of fasting. He answered each temptation of the devil by quoting the Scripture in rebuttal, "It is written. . . ."

We may wonder why God doesn't simply crush the power of the enemy himself, without using us. Since Satan used man to corrupt God's creation, it is only fitting that God's plan to overthrow Satan includes man. We are united with Jesus "In order that the manifold wisdom of God might now be made known through the church to the rulers and the authorities in the heavenly places" (Eph. 3:10). This was in accordance with the eternal purpose which He carried out in Christ Jesus our Lord who is seated at the right hand of the Father.

> Far above all rule and authority and power and dominion, and every name that is named, not only in this age, but also in the one to come. And He put all things in subjection under His feet, and gave Him as head over all things to the church, which is His body, the fulness of Him who fills all in all. (Eph. 1:21-23)

THREE
SPIRITUAL
WARFARE

In order to avoid becoming unbalanced in ministry, we must keep in mind that only an estimated ten percent of the problems we encounter will be demonic in nature. The other ninety percent will be of other causes. Many of man's compulsions stem from the fact that he does just what he wants to do; he likes to be the way he is. He justifies his bad behavior, words, and attitudes, attributing them to the way he is treated by those around him. In reality, no one forces him to be childishly ill-tempered or vindictive. No one has made him a depressed whiner or a pompous bully. He self-pityingly and self-righteously moves across the stage of life, loving the attention it brings, pretending martyrdom to a usually unimpressed, but often captive audience.

Although he insists that he would like to quit smoking, glutting himself, getting drunk, cursing, lusting, or blowing his stack, he secretly, though perhaps subconsciously, enjoys every delicious moment of what he does and wouldn't dream of stopping. This brother is walking in the fleshly drives of his carnal human nature and must face the truth about himself and repent. Occasionally, a sincere brother will repeatedly attempt exorcism as a remedy for his sin, not realizing that it is unsuccessful because he cannot cast out his own will.

The ministry of deliverance is intended to destroy the works of the devil and to set the captives free. If a brother is truly captive to a force outside of his control, then the minister must prescribe deliverance. Unfortunately, the devil gets the blame for much more than he actually does and people often hide behind the devil rather than accept the responsibility for their own attitudes and actions.

In this chapter we will address the issue of true demonic bondage. If a brother has tried with all his strength and resolve to change his ways, has confessed his faults, and with prayer and fasting made an earnest attempt to clean up his life but to no avail, then we can consider that he needs deliverance.

It is important for the one in need to realize that his help comes from the Lord Jesus Christ and only secondarily comes through the minister. If he does not know Jesus and has not given his life to the Lord, he should be led through the Scriptures to a saving knowledge of Jesus, openly declaring his faith.

> If thou shalt confess with thy mouth the Lord Jesus and shalt believe in thine heart that God hath raised him from the dead, thou shalt be saved. (Rom. 10:9, KJV)

The word in the Greek that is translated "saved" is *sozo*, which can also be translated to deliver, protect, heal, preserve, or to make whole. After the brother's deliverance, it is then appropriate to pray for him to be baptized in the Holy Spirit, in order to empower him to resist the return of those demons and to fill the void left by them (Matt. 12:43-45).

The recommended order of ministry is as follows:
1. Salvation
2. Water Baptism
3. Deliverance and Healing
4. Baptism in the Holy Spirit
5. Stirring up the gift of God and ministry within him.

When this sequence is not followed, problems can arise which could otherwise be avoided. In my own experience, I was first saved and baptized in the Holy Spirit; next I was baptized in water; then, after much conflict, I underwent deliverance.

Some people do not accept any part of the concept of demonic bondage. Rather, they believe that the only evil entity in the world is some sort of nebulous force which is devoid of any personality or involvement with individuals. These people float through their days in an "everything is beautiful" bubble. They do not recognize the realities of life or the Scriptures which clearly describe the fierce conflict between the Lord with His angels and saints, and Satan with his demonic cohorts. They persist in their concept of God as one who is a sort of Santa Claus, a jolly, good-natured deity who never chastises anyone, who would never let a demon come into anyone, who would never condemn anyone to hell. As a result of this kind of thinking, there has risen the false doctrine of ultimate reconciliation, which states that all created beings, including Satan and the fallen angels, will ultimately be saved and reconciled to God. This is clearly refuted in the Scriptures.

> And the devil who deceived them was thrown into the lake of fire and brimstone, where the beast and the false prophet are also; and they will be tormented day and night forever and ever. (Rev. 20:10) And if anyone's name was not found written in the book of life, he was thrown into the lake of fire. (Rev. 20:15)

A group of Christians who did not believe that God would allow a person to be demonically bound attended our meetings for a time. When they realized that we took the Scriptures literally concerning spiritual warfare, they left us and began their own meetings in East Miami. One of their leaders called me one evening while we were having a home prayer meeting and asked for help with a problem that they couldn't handle. When they had prayed for a young woman to be baptized in the Holy Spirit, she had begun to behave in a most bizarre manner, and they feared that she was going mad. She cursed them and threw herself about, totally out of control.

I told them to bring her over to my house. When they arrived, I saw that the woman was wild and could not be contained easily, so I dismissed the meeting. The woman was the daughter of a prominent public leader, and had been used by both her father and grandfather as a subject of hypnosis. She was also involved in witchcraft, had been raped as a child, and had many demonic problems. We prayed for her from 9:00 P.M. unitl about 4:00 A.M. when finally, she was set free. The next day, the woman called me on the telephone and asked me to come to her home to minister to the youngest of her five daughters because the girl was hearing voices.

Some of the East Miami group, Evelyn, and I went to her home. When we arrived, her little girl, whom I had never before met, came up to me and put her arms around me. I signaled to the mother, wordlessly asking her if this was the one, and she nodded yes. That little girl knew deep within her that I had come to help her, in somewhat the same way that the demoniac had recognized Jesus who had the power to set him free (Luke 8:28). We prayed for the child and commanded the voices to cease in Jesus' name. Then the house was exorcised and blessed and all members of the household were also blessed and dedicated to the Lord.

By now, the East Miami group had reversed their previous position. Because these brothers and sisters had heard with their own ears the demons speaking out of the woman's mouth, they now believed that a Christian could indeed need deliverance. Those who steadfastly believe that all of their internal conflicts are with self and that their external conflicts are with other people fail to understand that they are engaged in spiritual warfare.

> For we are not fighting against people made of flesh and blood, but against persons without bodies—the evil rulers of the unseen world, those mighty satanic beings and great evil princes of darkness, who rule this world; and against huge numbers of wicked spirits in the spirit world. (Eph. 6:12, TLB)

It is these wicked spirits who influence and direct much of the evil endeavors of humanity. When they pit a husband against wife, child against parent, racial group against racial group, or nation against nation, nobody wins except the forces of darkness, unless the people involved can recognize the work of the enemy, put on the whole armor of God (Eph. 6:11-17) and stand against the enemy in the name of Jesus.

Let us examine the nature of the enemy a little more closely. We read in Ezekiel about his beginnings and his fall from grace:

Thou has been in Eden the garden of God; every precious stone was thy covering . . . in the day that thou wast created. Thou art the anointed cherub that covereth; and I have set thee so: thou wast upon the holy mountain of God; thou hast walked up and down in the midst of the stones of fire. Thou wast perfect in thy ways from the day that thou wast created, till iniquity was found in thee. By the multitude of thy merchandise they have filled the midst of thee with violence, and thou has sinned: therefore I will cast thee as profane out of the mountain of God; and I will destroy thee, O covering chrub from the midst of the stones of fire. Thine heart was lifted up because of thy beauty, thou hast corrupted thy wisdom by reason of thy brightness: I will cast thee to the ground. . . . (Ezek. 28:13-17, KJB)

Isaiah gives us further insight into this fall:

How art thou fallen from heaven, O Lucifer, son of the morning! How are thou cut down to the ground which didst weaken the nations! For thou hast said in thine heart, I will ascend into heaven, I will exalt my throne above the stars of God: I will sit also upon the mount of the congregation, in the sides of the north: I will ascend above the heights of the clouds; I will be like the most high. Yet thou shalt be brought down to hell, to the sides of the pit. (Isa. 14:12-15, KJV)

Five times Lucifer says, "I will." The character of the devil and his demons is summed up in those words which express his pride and rebellion. The same attitude which Lucifer displayed is what gets us into trouble. By contrast, Jesus, when looking ahead to His suffering and death on the cross, said to the Father, "Not my will, but Thine be done" (Luke 22:42). Laying aside His divine nature, He took the form of a servant (Phil. 2:5-9), and further demonstrated His humility and obedience by stating that He only did the things which the Father showed Him to do (John 5:19).

We learn in the Scriptures that one third of all the angels fell to the earth with Lucifer after a great battle in heaven against Michael and the other angels of the Lord (Rev. 12:3, 4 and Rev. 12:7-9). Jesus refers to this when He explains the great advantage the disciples have over the enemy:

> And he said unto them, I beheld Satan as lightning fall from heaven. Behold, I give unto you power to tread on serpents and scorpions, and over all the power of the enemy: and nothing shall by any means hurt you. (Luke 10:18, 19, KJV)

This Scripture exhorts us to be fearless for we know that the Lord will stand by His word whenever we are sent by Him to rout out the enemy. In the general sense, we are given authority over unclean spirits and commanded to heal every kind of disease, raise the dead, and cleanse the lepers, ministering to others with the same generosity that the Lord has ministered to us (Matt. 10:1-9). However, we should listen carefully for specific directions from Him and not charge ahead of His orders into battle.

Sometimes an illness is caused by an evil spirit which must be cast out before a person can be healed. Before I realized this, I once prayed for a woman to be healed of deafness. During the following two weeks she could hear perfectly; but then, her hearing began to fade. She called me up to tell me that she was losing her hearing. I prayed for her over the phone and her hearing was restored for a few more days and then she began to lose it again. I prayed once more but nothing happened. I puzzled over this for a long time. Years later, the Lord showed me that a spirit of deafness had held the woman in bondage and because it had not been expelled, she received only temporary help. Now I know how to minister to a person in that condition.

On a recent trip up north, I prayed for a deaf woman. I expelled a spirit of deafness from her ears in the name of Jesus and told her, "Sister, take a deep breath and let it come out." She began to cough. Then I prayed for her healing. She fell to the floor and wept. The congregation began to applaud the Lord, because they discerned by the Spirit of the Lord that she had been set free and was healed even though she hadn't said a word. She told me afterward that something had popped in her ears and she had been able to hear instantly. Of course, there are times when all a minister has to do is lay his hands on the sick and they are healed; but other times, when an evil spirit is preventing their healing, they must first be delivered (Matt. 8:16, 17).

Occasionally a spirit will speak out of a brother and refuse to come out of him. The spirits consider him their house and don't want to leave. When the brother truly renounces them and they are commanded to leave in the name of Jesus, they must go. They will usually try to return, but the brother's safeguard against that is to turn that area of his life over to the Lord and invite the Holy Spirit in to replace that evil influence (Luke 11:20-26).

In recent years, the deception of reincarnation has become quite popular with hypnotists. They attempt to take a person back through his childhood, infancy, birth, gestation period, and conception, and supposedly into his previous life or lives, through the illicit practice of hypnosis. Under hypnosis, the subject "remembers" in detail, persons, places, and events. which, one assumes, he couldn't possibly have known unless he had been present in a previous life. Occasionally during deliverance, a minister will run into this kind of situation, but this is what has really happened: When a person who had hosted a demon dies, the demon will look for another to inhabit. He will bring with him into his new home all the memories of his existence in the former host. The demon, speaking out of the person during deliverance (or while the person is under hypnosis), will try to deceive those present into believing that the person had lived a previous life. That demonic lie is the basis for the so-called "evidence" of reincarnation. The evil spirit goes from body to body throughout the centuries, delighted when he can deceive people with the doctrine of reincarnation, which states that one atones for sins of former lives by good deeds performed in later lives. This doctrine does away with the efficacy of Jesus' atoning death on the cross (Heb. 10:10-14) and the promise we have that men will have to taste of death only once (Heb. 9:27).

Familiar spirits also manifest themselves through spiritualists or mediums. A spirit pretends to be a dear departed relative or friend, and through the medium gives out information that only the deceased had access to. Again, the information comes from a spirit that either inhabited the deceased or closely observed him during his life.

The minister of deliverance should not be concerned with where the demons go after they are cast out. The scriptural pattern we have is merely to cast them out of the person they are tormenting. The only exception to this is the one occasion in Mark 5:13 when Jesus permitted a legion of demons to leave the man and to enter a herd of swine which then rushed into the sea and drowned. An evil spirit, as it has been noted earlier, does not want to leave the person he is inhabiting. Often, when a spirit is cast out of a brother in the name of Jesus, it objects strongly and tries to hold onto him, screaming and tearing him as it is expelled (Mark 1:25-26). Usually the spirit leaves with a visible manifestation of coughing, burping, crying, sneezing, or yawning; that is, in an act of expelling the breath. The word for breath and spirit are the same in the Greek, *pnuema*.

A minister who becomes experienced in deliverance will become known in the spirit world, and the demons will recognize him in the same way that they recognized Paul in Acts 19:15. Once I was praying for a line of people after our regular Friday evening service when a man stepped up for prayer who had a reputation for being violent. When I laid my hands on him, he immediately jumped back and assumed a karate stance. I said, "The blood of Jesus, between you and me!" At that he went on a rampage throughout the dance studio where we held our services, hitting and breaking the railings with his hands and plunging his fist through the wall. His violent strength could easily have killed somebody, but we followed after him and bound the spirits of karate and violence in the name and by the blood of Jesus; and the man fell to the floor. We then cast those spirits out and he was set free.

Most of the martial arts from eastern cultures are demonically inspired. Many of them openly acknowledge a false god as their source of inspiration and strength. Any brother who is engaged in one of these eastern practices should check out its origin, as it is likely that he is engaged in a ritual which ensnares its participants by means of the evil principality over it.

There are eight requirements for deliverance to be effective and permanent:

1. Acknowledge Jesus as Lord and Savior.
2. Honest acknowledgment of sin—"I acknowledged my sin to Thee, and my iniquity I did not hide; I said, 'I will confess my transgressions to the Lord'; and Thou didst forgive the guilt of my sin." (Ps. 32:5)
3. Humility—". . . God is opposed to the proud, but gives grace to the humble. Submit therefore to God. Resist the devil and he will flee from you." (James 4:6, 7)
4. Remorse—"And there you will remember your ways and all your deeds, with which you have defiled yourselves; and you will loathe yourselves in your own sight for all the evil things that you have done." (Ezek. 20:43)
5. Repentance—"Therefore bring forth fruit in keeping with your repentance." (Matt. 3:8)

Paul amplifies on how this is to be done in the fourth and fifth chapters of his letter to the Ephesians:

a. Laying aside falsehood, speak truth to one another.
b. Do not give the devil an opportunity through your anger, but make peace with one another before the end of the day.
c. Let the thief steal no more, but rather, let him perform honest labor, earning enough to be able to share with those in need.
d. Put aside unwholesome communications, speaking only those things which edify the listeners.
e. Put away all bitterness, wrath, anger, slander, malice, and noisy demands or complaints. Instead, be kind to one another, tender-hearted and forgiving.
f. Do not walk in immorality, impurity, or greed, but walk in unselfish love.
g. No longer jest or talk in a silly or filthy manner, but let your words express thankfulness.
h. Do not be immoral, impure, covetous, disobedient or an idolater; rather, walk as children of light in goodness, righteousness, and truth.
i. Do not participate in secret sins, but instead, expose them.
j. Do not walk in darkness, but try to learn what is pleasing to the Lord.
k. Do not get drunk with wine, but be filled with the Holy Spirit.

6. Forgiveness—"For if you forgive men for their transgressions, your heavenly Father will also forgive you. But if you do not forgive men, then your Father will not forgive your transgressions. (Matt. 6:14, 15)

7. Reaching out to the Lord for help—"And it will come about that whoever calls on the name of the Lord will be delivered." (Joel 2:32)

8. Recognize that we have the victory in our spiritual warfare—"Behold, I have given you authority to tread upon serpents and scorpions, and over all the power of the enemy, and nothing shall injure you." (Luke 10:19)

If the brother is willing to comply with these eight requirements, the minister will be successful in delivering him. In the next chapter we will explain step by step how to conduct a deliverance session.

FOUR
ORDER OF
DELIVERANCE

When a brother calls to make an appointment for deliverance, he is often emotionally prepared; however, he may not be scripturally enlightened about spiritual warfare. Before praying for the brother, I recommend and often insist that he listen to my taped series on deliverance and healing so that he may become prepared in these ways;

1. to learn about Jesus, his Savior and Deliverer.
2. to understand how he might have opened himself up to evil spirits.
3. to anticipate the victory which Jesus has obtained for him.
4. to prepare his heart for a repentant life.
5. to know what to expect during the deliverance session.
6. to be able to deliver himself in the future from any demonic bondage which he might discern.
7. to be able to prevent the return of the demons once he has been set free.
8. to be able to help any of his brothers or sisters in their need.

The brother must see the necessity of regular fellowship because he needs the safety and the life-flow that comes from the body of Christ. He also is encouraged to feed upon the Word of God as his main source of sustenance. If he has not already been baptized in the Holy Spirit, he is encouraged to seek that blessing in order to be empowered against the enemy's subterfuge.

The brother is then invited to come to my office for prayer, counseling and whatever deliverance he might need. The first thing we do is recognize the presence of the Lord and worship Him together. We (most of the time, Evelyn and I minister together) then ask the Lord to give us a word of knowledge, a word of wisdom and discerning of spirits. After opening this appointment time with prayer, we are ready to begin.

I usually ask the brother to tell us about himself, beginning in his early childhood. His early relationships with his mother and father are quite often a source of problem and bondage to him. We ask him to recall any traumatic experiences or any negative emotions, such as rejection. We ask him if he was an unwanted child or if he was illegitimate. As the brother talks about his past, I jot down anything which the Holy Spirit reveals to me. When the brother is finished with his story, I lead him in a prayer of faith, making sure that he knows that he is saved. I request that he repeat the following after me:

General Confession of Faith

Lord Jesus Christ, I believe that you are the Son of God. You are the Messiah, come in the flesh, to destroy the works of the devil. You died on the cross for my sins and rose again from the dead. I now confess all my sins and repent. I ask you to forgive me and cleanse me in your blood. I believe that your blood cleanses me now from all sins. Thank you for redeeming me, cleansing me, justifying me, and sanctifying me in your blood.

During the remainder of the session, I utilize the information gathered in the interview as I lead the brother through the following prayers. These prayers are said basically in order and usually precipitate the actual deliverance.

The next prayer relates to the brother's beginnings. At various points during this prayer, the Holy Spirit will begin to bring release to the brother and he may weep or manifest in another way the particular spirit which had held him in bondage. Often the Holy Spirit will give us a word specifying the demonic sources of the problem. After we have dealt with that demon, we pray for healing in that area and continue the prayer where we had left off. The minister should watch for common trouble spots, such as whether the brother's parents were disappointed that the baby turned out to be a boy. The minister should stop at any point where he discerns a demon or where the brother remembers an incident which could have provided entry for a demon.

Healing of a Wounded Spirit

Dear Heavenly Father, Lord Jesus, Holy Spirit, you were there when I was conceived in my mother's womb. You knew whether I was conceived in love or in lust. Heal me now of all that was not of you, that came in at that time of my life. Even if my father or mother did reject me at that time of my life, you will never reject me. You loved me all during the time I was being formed in my mother's womb. Deliver me from all loneliness, fear of pregnancy, rejection, feeling unwanted, unneeded, and unloved. Free me from any demonic bondage which entered me as a result of an attempted abortion or any other negative thing which may have entered me while I was being formed in my mother's womb. Heavenly Father, you were there when I was born. Let me now know that you received me and loved me at that time of my life. Though my father or mother may have rejected me, yet you never did, neither when I was born, nor at any other period of my life. Father, please heal now all the wounds of rejection, all the hurts, all the wounds of the past, whether or not I remember them. Heal my wounded and bruised spirit, my broken heart—whether this occurred as a new-born baby, a small child, a teenager, a young adult, or as a mature person. Thank you for loving me, Father, I offer this prayer in the name of Jesus.

As a result of wounds suffered in his past, the brother may have much to forgive. We lead him in the following prayer, stopping at any time we discern that he is bound by a spirit of unforgiveness, and we cast it out of him. This may be the time we discern a spirit of hatred of father or mother, a spirit of bitterness, or resentment, or murder. We cast any of these out, also, in the name of Jesus.

Forgiveness Prayer

Lord, I have a confession to make. I have not loved but have resented certain people and have unforgiveness in my heart. I ask you to forgive me for this. I call upon you, Lord, to help me to forgive them. I do now forgive (name them both living and dead) and ask you to forgive them also. I accept and forgive myself for all my shortcomings.

Many people have been involved in the occult, which is a form of idolatry, and this may be another of the brother's problems. He may have played with a Ouija board, read his horoscope, gone to seances, or to a fortuneteller. He may have been involved with hypnotism, divination, necromancy, familiar spirits, tarot cards, handwriting analysis, Hare Krishna, witchcraft, or the writings of Jeanne Dixon or Edgar Cayce. The brother may have been in Satan worship or another cult such as Christian Science, Jehovah's Witnesses, Mormonism, or any other religion which does not teach the same about Jesus Christ as Paul taught. Paul speaks strongly about these false teachings:

. . . There are some who are disturbing you, and want to distort the gospel of Christ. But even though we, or an angel from heaven, should preach to you a gospel contrary to that which we have preached to you, let him be accursed. (Gal. 1:7, 8)

These practices and religions should be renounced by the brother before the following prayer:

Occult Confession Prayer

Lord, I now confess that I sought from Satan the help that should only come from God. I confess as sin (name every one of the occult sins he has been in) and also those sins I cannot remember. Lord, I now repent and renounce these sins and ask you to forgive me. I renounce Satan and all his works. I hate his demons. I count them all my enemies. In the name of Jesus Christ, I now close the door on all occult practices, and I command all such spirits to leave me now in the name of Jesus Christ. (At this time each of the spirits behind the brother's occult practices should be commanded to leave him in Jesus' name.)

In the Scriptures, we read that a person of illegitimate birth cannot enter the assembly of the Lord, nor can any of his descendants for ten generations (Deut. 23:2). It is possible that the stigma of illegitimate birth can be carried to future generations through an evil spirit. If the brother's ancestors are of a specific ethnic group or nationality, such as, Indian, Italian, Chinese, or Gypsy, there may be certain evil spirits which may affect each group and which may have been passed down to him. For example, I once ministered to a man of Indian descent who periodically found himself strongly hating his wife without any reason. When he went through deliverance, the Holy Spirit showed us that he was being influenced by an evil spirit which caused this Indian to hate his paleface wife, even to the point of desiring to kill and scalp her. In the next prayer we cover this kind of situation.

Loosing From Domination

In the name of Jesus Christ I now renounce all bondages, break and loose myself from all demonic subjection to my mother, father, grandparents, or any other human beings, living or dead, who have dominated me in any way. I command every evil spirit that has come into my family line, even back through the tenth generation, out of me in Jesus' name. And I thank you, Lord, for setting me free.

At the conclusion of the following prayer, we command all spirits to leave which could have affected the brother's mind, such as: confusion, mind control, mind binding, insanity, fear of insanity, madness, violent rage, murder, fantasy, coveteousness, schizophrenia, doublemindedness, or counterfeit personality.

Psychic Heredity and Bondage Prayer

In the name of Jesus Christ, I now renounce every evil bondage, break and loose myself and my children from all psychic powers or bondages or bonds of physical or mental illness, put upon me or my family line due to my parents or any other ancestor, even back to the tenth generation. I thank you, Lord Jesus, for setting me free.

I usually preface the next prayer, by instructing the brother as we go through the list, to let me know if anything begins to shake, move, or tremble within him at the mention of any particular bondage. At the conclusion of the prayer, we lead the brother in a specific prayer of renunciation to take back any ground ever yielded to Satan. Then we take authority over any spirit which has manifested itself in any way commanding it to leave.

Loosing of Curses, Spells, etc., Prayer

In the name of Jesus Christ I now rebuke any evil spirits, breaking their power, and loose myself and my children, from any and all evil curses, charms, hexes, spells, jinxes, psychic powers, bewitchment, witchcraft, sorcery, incantation, impartations, or assignments that have been put upon me or my family line from any person or persons, living or dead, or from any occult or psychic sources (including a familiar spirit assigned to me by Satan at my birth, to try to lead me astray all my life), or due to my own sins. I rebuke all connected and related spirits and command them to leave me in Jesus' name.

This next prayer precedes a general renunciation of various types of evil influences:

Recommitment to Jesus, my Deliverer

I come to you, Jesus, as my deliverer. You know all my problems (name them), all the things that bind, torment, defile and harass me. I now loose myself from every dark spirit, from every evil influence, from every satanic bondage, from every spirit in me that is not the Spirit of God, and I command all such spirits to leave me, now, in the name of Jesus Christ. I now confess that my body is a temple for the Holy Spirit, redeemed, cleansed, sanctified, by the blood of Jesus. Therefore, Satan has no place, no power over me, because of the blood of Jesus.

Following this prayer, we go into a general cleansing of all common areas of sin and potential bondage. For example, fear of one kind or another usually torments every individual that needs deliverance. I ask the brother to name any specific fears that he might have, such as: fear of heights, fear of the dark, fear of being suffocated, fear of being closed in, fear of driving a car on the expressway, fear of being alone, fear of people, fear of being unloved, fear of sickness, fear of cancer, or fear of rejection. Whatever his fears are, I ask the brother to renounce each by name and command the spirit to leave in the name of Jesus.

Usually we find that related groups of evil spirits will enter an individual. If the brother has been bound by fear, he quite often will be in bondage to a spirit of worry, anxiety, self-pity, guilt, self-condemnation, discouragement, defeatism, hopelessness, loneliness, depression, suicide, and/or death. A person with a low self-image may have a spirit of insecurity, self-rejection, nail-biting, bed-wetting and thumb-sucking. These spirits often accompany a spirit of rejection. When we cast out the ruling spirit, we also command each of its kindred spirits to untie themselves from each other and to leave the brother.

The next general area we deal with is the realm of unbelief. Doubt, skepticism, and cynicism are often companion spirits of unbelief. The category of pride is next, along with its kindred spirits of egotism, self-righteousness, vanity, contention, and quarreling. The next grouping is headed by a spirit of rebellion which is likened to witchcraft in the Scriptures and the related spirits, antichrist and idolatry.

God created us to be sexual beings and the enemy tries to pervert and destroy this part of God's plan for his children any way he can. The next groups are in the realm of the sins of the flesh, the chief of which is lust, and is often accompanied by adultery, fornication, fantasy-lust, and masturbation. In a case where a girl has been sexually molested, she may be bound by a spirit of rape. If this has happened, then other accompanying spirits would be fear of man, uncleanness, shame, frigidity, fear of sex, hatred of sex, and incest. If this girl marries, she might also need to be delivered from a spirit of fear of husband. After the girl or woman is delivered from all tormenting spirits which entered her as a result of her being molested, she must forgive the person who attacked her. Otherwise, these spirits will have the authority to remain in her (Matt. 18:34, 35). We ask the Lord to minister healing to her, removing every scar produced by the memory of the terror and pain of that event.

Abortion heads the next classification of demons. This includes murder, spirit of child-sacrifice, the spirit of Baal, and the spirit of Molech. Sexual bondages which can be grouped under sodomy are homosexuality and lesbianism with their accompanying practices of oral sex and sadomasochism.

There are sexual spirits that go along with certain occult practices or ceremonies such as the black mass and orgies. Women who have been prostitutes may have to be delivered of spirits of harlotry, whoredom and a Jezebel spirit. These and other spirits of perversion, such as beastiality, can enter a person even if his sin was only mental and was not physically committed.

The Holy Spirit will give discernment about other demonic bondages such as stubbornness (which 1 Sam. 15:23 likens to idolatry), jealousy, religious pride, and other religious spirits.

Other groupings would be the spirits attached to untruth such as lying spirits, slander, gossip, blasphemy, blabbermouth, and those which have to do with compulsive habits such as alcoholism, smoking, drugs, and dope. Each addicting spirit should be named specifically, renounced, and cast out individually. Also, a general spirit of addiction should be cast out so that it won't cause the person to substitute another kind of addiction for the one which has been renounced. Related to this group are the spirits of gluttony, self-indulgence, obesity, compulsion, and fat.

There are spirits of infirmity which can cause every sickness and physical abnormality known to man. We do not believe that all sickness is caused by an evil spirit, but whenever it is, that illness can be cured by casting out that particular spirit of the affected individual. Even if the person has no symptoms of illness, the Holy Spirit may indicate that he has a spirit which plans to manifest that illness in the future, especially if other members of his family have it or have had it. After deliverance we pray for the healing of any condition which had been caused by a demon.

If the brother or sister has been delivered before of the same spirits which are now being discerned, it may be necessary to break a soul-tie. For example, if a brother had sexual relations with a woman who was not his wife, that person becomes one with him (1 Cor. 6:16). He may have a recurrent problem with an unclean spirit until the soul-tie between him and that woman is broken. If this is the case, I lead the brother in breaking the soul-tie with any person out of his past which would hinder his Christian walk and growth. We come against any ungodly soul-ties and renounce and forsake them all individually. The brother declares that he is cleansed by the blood of the Lamb. He affirms all legitimate soul-ties to wife and family and to the liberated body of Christ.

At the close of the deliverance session, we ask the Holy Spirit to come into the brother's life and fill every area which had formerly been held captive by the enemy (Matt. 12:43-45). We instruct the brother how to put on the full armor of God (Eph. 6:10-18) in order to be able to withstand any attempt of demonic powers to enter and dominate his life in the future. I request that the brother raise his hands and begin to worship the Lord in tongues. In the event that he has not been baptized in the Holy Spirit or has never before prayed in tongues, I show him how to yield to the Lord so that he might be both filled with the Holy Spirit and be able to pray in this way. Usually, after deliverance, a person will have a greater freedom in doing this.

Before the brother leaves my office, I instruct him in the following essentials for keeping his deliverance.

Essentials for Retaining Deliverance

1. Put on the full armor of God. (Eph. 6:10-18)
2. Make a positive confession of faith. (Mark 11:22-24)
3. Stay in the Scriptures. (Ps. 1:1-3)
4. Crucify the flesh. (Luke 9:23-25)
5. Communicate with the Lord, especially in praising Him. (Ps. 100)
6. Keep in fellowship and be submitted to the body of Christ. (Heb. 10:24, 25; 13:17)

7. Totally commit yourself to Jesus Christ. (Matt. 22:37 and John 12:26)

As the Scripture tells us, if we walk in the Spirit, we will not fulfill the lusts of the flesh (Gal. 5:16). In a later chapter we will be into more detail on how to keep our healing and deliverance.

FIVE
CHILDREN'S
DELIVERANCE

Whether ministering on a one-to-one basis or in a group setting, deliverance for children is similar to deliverance for adults. Initially, we get acquainted and establish a relaxed atmosphere. Instructions are given both to the children and to the parents. Questions are directed to them to stimulate an examination of conscience and to find out if they have already observed areas of bondage in their lives. Then, we go into the deliverance itself. All of our remarks should be aimed at the level of understanding of the youngest present, using the appropriate vocabulary for that age's ability to comprehend.

At the beginning of a group session, we address our first remarks to the parents. It is very important for the parents to undergo deliverance before they bring their children to be delivered. In fact, it is sometimes impossible for the child to be set free unless his parent or parents is first set free. On one such occasion, I prayed for a young girl who was held captive by a spirit of masturbation. When I attempted to cast that demon out, it refused to budge, and the girl's legs, hands, and fingers became stiff and painful. The child screamed continuously until one of the ministers in charge of the deliverance service directed me to carry her outside. I brought her out to her parents and explained to them what had happened. Then, the girl's father took me aside and confided to me that he had the same problem of masturbation that his little girl had. After the father was delivered, we were able to cast the evil spirit out of his daughter.

I firmly believe that it is the responsibility of the parents, the fathers in particular, to bring their children to Jesus, not only for salvation, but also for healing and deliverance. Many Christian men try to delegate this responsibility to others, such as pastors, Sunday school teachers, or even to their wives, but the Scripture is clear. It is the fathers who are admonished to bring up their children in the discipline and instruction of the Lord (Eph. 6:4). I don't mean to imply that the mother is prohibited from leading her children in the ways of the Lord, but the primary responsibility lies with the father and only secondarily with the mother. Ideally, it should be a team effort. Both their lives should be lived in front of their children in such an exemplary way as to motivate their children to see the Lord in every situation and to follow Him. However, in the case of a family where only one parent is a believer, it is the believing parent that consecrates the children, whether it is the father or the mother (1 Cor. 7:14). Fathers are directed in Ephesians 6:4 not to provoke their children to wrath. The consquences of stumbling a child are severe (Matt. 18:6) and parents cannot take their responsibilities lightly to provide the right environment with godly examples of attitude and behavior.

Parents have the authority to believe on their child's behalf when a child does not or cannot have faith for himself:

> And they brought the boy to Him. And when he saw Him, immediately the spirit threw him into a convulsion, and falling to the ground, he began rolling about and foaming at the mouth. And He asked his father, "How long has this been happening to him?" And he said, "From childhood. And it has often thrown him both into the fire and into the water to destroy him. But if you can do anything, take pity on us and help us!" And Jesus said to him, "If You can! All things are possible to him who believes." Immediately the boy's father cried out and began saying, "I do believe; help me in my unbelief." (Mark 9:20-24)

If the parents do not have the faith that their child can be helped, then most likely, the child will not be helped. Parents must come to the Lord believing that He can and will hear their cry, and that all things are possible with God. Like the father in Mark 9, if a parent has insufficient faith, let him ask God to supply whatever is lacking (Gal. 2:20).

After instructing the parents, the children are addressed. Although God holds parents responsible for their sinful neglect and bad example to their children, children who are candidates for deliverance must realize that they themselves are responsible for their own actions, increasingly as they grow older. They should understand that the day will come when they are fully accountable to God for their sins and can no longer blame their government or parents for failing them. God speaks to them in Ephesians 6:1-3.

> Children, obey your parents in the Lord, for this is right. Honor your father and mother (which is the first commandment with a promise), That it may be well with you, and that you may live long on the earth.

The Lord does not say to obey parents only if they are right or kindly. Some children justify disobedience to parents on the grounds that their parents are ungodly, or unjust, or unreasonable, or ignorant, or unloving, or unfair. Nevertheless, the commandment says simply to obey and honor them without any qualification. The children should be instructed that disobedience to parents is a sin and they must repent of all sin if they want God to hear their prayers. Then, the children can expect God to answer their requests for any necessary changes in their parents (2 Cor. 10:6).

The minister should instruct the children in very simple terms about Jesus bringing salvation, healing, and deliverance to the earth. They should be made to realize that we are engaged in spiritual warfare with our enemy, the devil, and that Jesus has provided us with the means of overcoming the devil. The story of Jesus' fasting and temptation in the desert (Luke 4:1-13) is a good one to use for this purpose. Their confidence in the Lord's protection should be built so that they will not be afraid (Luke 10:19).

The minister of deliverance should keep in mind that the evil spirits which afflict children are just as deadly as those which afflict adults. Any demonic presence that is discerned in a child should not be ignored until a time when the child is older and "can understand what is going on." The longer a person has an evil spirit, the stronger a grip it will have on him, the more it will entice him to accept other evil influences into his life, and the harder it will become for him to repent and turn that area of his life over to Jesus.

When addressing the demons in children, it is not always necessary for the children to understand the exact nature of the problem; the demons know what you are talking about and know that they must leave the children when you cast them out. Except in the cast of an infant who will comprehend nothing, it is usually sufficient for a child to understand merely that he is rejecting evil and turning to the Lord Jesus.

After deliverance is over, the parents and children are instructed how to keep their deliverance. The main emphasis should be placed upon their relationship with Jesus and faith in His Word. Jesus said that we must be converted and become as little children in order to enter the kingdom of heaven, and that the greatest one in the kingdom of heaven was one who would humble himself as a child (Matt. 18:3, 4). The minister of deliverance must keep this in mind as he wields the sword of the Spirit, lest he become puffed up because of his many victories over the enemy.

SIX
TOTAL HEALING

In the beginning, God placed the tree of life in the garden of Eden among the other trees. He told Adam that he might eat of the fruit of all the trees, including the tree of life, with the exception of the tree of the knowledge of good and evil (Gen. 2:16, 17). After Adam and Eve were banished from the garden because of their disobedience, the Lord "stationed the cherubim and the flaming sword which turned every direction to guard the way to the tree of life" (Gen. 3:24). He did not want Adam and Eve, in their fallen condition, to eat from the tree of life and live forever (Gen. 3:22). With the exception of four metaphoric references in Proverbs where wisdom, the fruit of the righteous, desire fulfilled, and a soothing tongue are likened to the tree of life, we hear no further mention of it until, at the culmination of this age, in the very last book of the Bible, the overcomers are told that the Lord will grant them to eat from the tree of life (Rev. 2:7).

> And he showed me a river of the water of life, clear as crystal, coming from the throne of God and of the Lamb, in the middle of its street. And on either side of the river was the tree of life, bearing twelve kinds of fruit, yielding its fruit every month; and the leaves of the tree were for the healing of the nations. (Rev. 22:1-2)

We find in Revelations 22:14 that those who have washed their robes in the blood of the Lamb have the right to the tree of life. Although we may not understand the full significance of all these passages, we may draw at least one conclusion from them: by the fall of man, we lost our right to any benefit from the tree of life, but by our obedience to cleanse ourselves in the blood of Jesus, we can regain that loss. In this chapter we will take a closer look at the healing which is to be found in the tree of life. We will divide healing into four categories: the healing of physical afflictions; healing of demonic afflictions; inner healing, that is, the healing of scars and wounds from emotional experiences, and healing of souls from the effect of sin.

1. *Healing of the Soul*

The most life-changing of these four groupings is that healing of the soul which occurs when we repent of our sin and turn to Jesus as Lord of our lives. "As for me, I said, 'O Lord, be gracious to me; heal my soul, for I have sinned against Thee'" (Ps. 41:4).

This begins at the point of our conversion and continues throughout our lives as we give up the carnal, humanistic ways of our old nature and yield to the Lord with our new Christ-like nature whenever our will conflicts with His. True repentance carries with it a hatred for anything we might say, do, or think which would be repugnant to God.

> And there you will remember your ways and all your deeds, with which you have defiled yourselves; and you will loathe yourselves in your own sight for all the evil things that you have done. (Ez. 20:43)

In 1967, after I had sought for two or three months to be baptized in the Holy Spirit, my daughter and her husband invited Evelyn and me to accompany them and their four daughters to Gerald Derstine's Christian Retreat Camp in Minnesota. While at camp, several people prayed for me to receive the Holy Spirit, but there seemed to be some sort of a block. As I walked about the room praying, the people repeatedly instructed me to keep my hands up in the air. I felt rather foolish doing this, but I complied. Then, as I walked about, praying, the Lord's voice came to me saying that I should rebuke the devil who was trying to prevent me from receiving the Holy Spirit. At that, I rebuked the devil. As soon as I did, I was released and began to worship the Lord in tongues. I began to laugh, cry, and jump around the room, clapping my hands and going around the room kissing and hugging every man, woman, and child there. I just loved them all. That wasn't me and I knew it!

After I finally got to sleep that night in our motel room, I was awakened by a voice and a sound like the beating of a bass drum. The voice called my name, "Frank!" I got up and went to the window, but couldn't see anyone. I opened the door and looked out but there was no one there. Returning to my bed, I concluded that I had heard sounds from one of the other motel rooms. As I pulled up the covers, the voice called to me again, "Frank, get on your knees." Then I knew who it was. It was my heaveny Father calling me to repentance. As I knelt by the side of my bed, He showed me my life as vividly as if I were watching a television screen. I saw all the things I ever did to dishonor my Father in heaven. I wept until the floor was wet with my tears as I reviewed the sins of my past. I hated what I had done and hated what I had been. After that, I felt that a great weight was lifted off me and I knew that my sins were not only forgiven, but also forgotten, no longer to be remembered and held against me by God.

In the account of David and Bathsheba we can see demonstrated just how complete God's forgiveness is for the repentant sinner. Although David and Bathsheba suffered the consequences of adultery by the loss of their son who was conceived out of wedlock, it is through their lineage that the Messiah was brought into this world (Matt. 1:6-17). If God could forgive them and use them to bring us the Lord Jesus Christ, then you and I can expect that His forgiveness will heal our souls and restore us to fellowship with Him.

The minister of reconciliation, who leads others to repentance and a saving knowledge of Jesus, is spoken of in metaphor: "The fruit of the righteous is a tree of life, and he who is wise wins souls" (Prov. 11:30).

We find in this aspect of healing, the restoration of relationship not only of God and man but of all human relationships.

We now have access to the tree of life whose leaves are for the healing of the nations.

2. Inner Healing

Now that we are reconciled to God and our souls are cleansed by the blood of the Lamb, we are able to receive God's comfort and healing for the wounds and afflictions in the inner person. Psalm 147:3 tells us that the Lord heals the brokenhearted and binds up their sorrows. We all can identify with David as he cries out that one has pierced his heart within him (Ps. 109:22) because we have all suffered rejection and hurts inflicted both intentionally and unintentionally by others.

Sometimes a painful experience is so difficult to bear that it is buried and blocked out of the memory. It cannot be faced so it is suppressed. We are no longer conscious that a wound still exists but, nevertheless, it will affect us in some tangible way— perhaps by our being defensive or overly sensitive or fearful in certain situations, or irritated, or even by our becoming physically ill. We read in Proverbs 15:4 that a soothing tongue is a tree of life, but a tongue which is perverted will crush the spirit. how many of us have ever said hurtful, cutting words which inflicted pain deep within another person? The soothing tongue of those who would minister healing can speak words of truth, reconciliation, and comfort to one who has been injured in this way. "The spirit of a man can endure his sickness, but a broken spirit who can bear?" (Prov. 18:14).

Internal stresses and wounds can so deeply sadden a person's heart that his spirit is broken (Prov. 15:13), and he will lack that spark which makes life worth living.

Recently, I received a letter from a young German woman whom I shall call Magda. She related her story to me: When her mother learned that she was pregnant with Magda, her father didn't want the pregnancy to continue because of the war. She remembers feeling rejected continually as a child. She stated that her older brother was better than her in every way. As she reached adulthood, Magda entered into several relationships with men, all with bad results. Magda cared for men but was extremely fearful of them and her heart was broken many times, leaving many scars on her memory. Although she had held unforgiveness and bitterness toward men in the past, she had not forgiven them.

About three years ago, she became ill at the time of a dispute with her mother over her inheritance. The doctors were uncertain if she had multiple sclerosis or rheumatoid arthritis. She and her mother hadn't communicated with each other for two years but were recently reconciled. Magda went to visit her in Germany and soon her mother is coming to the United States to visit her.

Magda has had three bad marriages: the first was to a man who turned out to be a homosexual; the second was to an alcoholic; the third, to an alcoholic who also smoked marijuana. This most recent marriage had ended in divorce two years ago. Magda had two abortions but had asked God to forgive her as she now realized that this was wrong. There were times when she was unable to cope with her problems and she asked God to take her from this world as she wanted to die.

All her life Magda felt the lack of love and attention. She felt unwanted and rejected. She generally feared people in much the same way that she had feared her parents. She was unable to fight for herself, to stand up and speak up for her rights. She felt uncertain, lost, and unhappy most of the time. She felt that she was a failure.

Magda said that she had listened to some of my taped messages. She wrote to thank me for them because they had helped her to get "close to God." She stated that she was now able to see things that she had been unable to see before, and that every day she was learning more about God and His Word. Now, she is able to admit to her sin, to experience God's forgiveness, and to forgive others. As Magda said at the close of her letter, "Life is so beautiful when you follow His direction."

Thank God for His comfort to the broken in heart and spirit! Here, the soothing tongue of Proverbs 15:4 pours out a balm of love to the afflicted even through the impersonal ministry of a taped sermon. Magda's deep-seated problem of rejection began even before she was born. However, when she learned the truth about God's love and acceptance of her, even though she was unwanted by mother, father, brother, friend, and husband, she was set free.

Even before birth, a child can feel the pangs of emotional starvation stemming from lack of parental love and acceptance. In a few cases, I have ministered to mothers who had unsuccessfully tried to abort their pregnancies. After they were delivered from spirits of abortion and murder, I instructed them to pray at night over their sleeping children and to ask God to heal the wounds they had inflicted by their extreme rejection of them. These mothers are further instructed to command the spirits of death, murder, and abortion to leave their children in the name of Jesus.

Often, a present problem will have its roots in the problems of childhood. A woman may be frigid toward her husband because of being wounded in some way by her father when she was a child; or a husband may have hostility toward his wife because, when he was a young boy, his mother was abusive toward him. When this is the case, the minister of inner healing should pray for brother (or sister) to receive from the Lord Jesus all the comfort, acceptance, and love which he discerns was needed at the time when the wounds were inflicted.

A young woman came to us for counseling while we were ministering out west. She was suffering from depression and various physical ailments. When Evelyn and I prayed for her, the Lord showed me a little white house with columns in front of it. I asked, "Sister, when you were a child, did you live in a little white house?" She answered that she had. I told her that something had happened in that house that was at the root of her problems, and she started to weep. I asked her what had happened. She said, "My daddy sent me out to the store and when I came back, the door was locked. I looked in the window and I saw my sister being raped by my daddy. She was crying and yelling; and I was banging on the door and banging and banging! I could kill him! I could kill him!"

When the woman calmed down, I asked her if she were willing to forgive her father even though he had done such a terrible thing to her sister. I instructed her that if her father should repent, that God would forgive him. If we don't forgive, we put ourselves above God. I asked her again if she were willing to forgive. She responded, "I can't forgive him!" "Then, I told her, "I can't help you."

Later on, thank God, she returned to us and said that she had changed her mind and that she would forgive her father. Because of the years of resentment and hatred she had borne toward her father, she had found it impossible to relate to any man. She had hated her several husbands, whom she had divorced, and had even hated God. This had produced the deep depression and other problems which caused her to ask us for prayer and counseling.

3. Physical Healing

It is becoming increasingly evident that many physical illnesses which were once believed to be strictly organic problems are actually produced by stress. Although the cause of physical infirmities is not always natural, whatever the cause, all healing comes from God. We can praise God that He has designed our bodies to self-heal in many ways: blood will clot in a cut or bruise and the wound will seal over; broken bones, when aligned properly, will mend back together again; foreign objects, such as splinters and thorns, are rejected and pushed out of the body. God has given us immunities to protect us from many irritants and organisms which might otherwise make us ill. If we do become ill, we have built-in fighters called antibodies which overcome and subdue the invaders and then we get well again. Medical science has made many wonderful discoveries about how the human body works. Doctors have learned to use the chemicals and elements which God has created to facilitate healing; and yet, there is a need still unmet by either modern medicine or the self-healing body.

We read both in the Old and New Testaments that Jesus bore our infirmities and that by the wounds He suffered as He was beaten, we are healed (1 Pet. 2:24 and Isa. 53:5). Here we have an avenue of healing which is not dependent upon the knowledge of man but upon the grace of God. Not that we should shun the natural remedy, but we must recognize that its ability to heal is God's design.

Let us be led by the Lord to whatever means of healing He should designate in each particular case. The minister of healing should recognize the sovereignty of God and the conscience of the individual in these matters as well as his own discernment, since it is by faith through grace that we are saved, healed, and delivered.

The minister of healing should be intimately familiar with the various ways in which healing is administered throughout the New Testament. For example, when called to minister to Peter's mother-in-law, Jesus rebuked the fever. In my own ministry, when praying for someone with a fever, I follow this precedent and rebuke the fever, commanding it to go in the name of Jesus Christ. It has been our experience that cancer is often of demonic origin and so, just as Jesus cursed the fig tree, we curse the cancer in His name, that it will wither and leave the body.

In James 4:3 we read, "You ask and receive not because ye ask amiss" (KJV). We must learn how to ask according to His Word, using the various methods demonstrated in His Word. We should know, for example about the prayer cloths described in Acts 19:11, 12, where extraordinary miracles were worked when handkerchiefs and aprons were taken from Paul and brought to the sick and the diseases left them and evil spirits went out of them. Some readers of the Bible may think that this is so much mumbo jumbo superstition, but what the Scripture says is true. We know that a piece of cloth is powerless, but coupled with faith in the Word of God and the examples given to us by the early disciples, we can use such a method of bringing healing or deliverance to an individual. We have often prayed that the Lord would use this point of contact and honor His Word and our prayers have been answered. God is not limited to any method. Even when we cannot be present with the one in need, God will still answer the prayer of faith.

There are occasions when God directs us to call for the elders of the church:

> Is anyone among you sick? Let him call for the elders of the church, and let them pray over him, anointing him with oil in the name of the Lord; and the prayer offered in faith will restore the one who is sick. . . . (James 5:14, 15)

Authority to pray an effective prayer for healing has been given to the elders and is part of their responsibility to the church. There are individuals who might find it difficult to submit to their elders; but if they will submit to that authority, God will indeed honor his Word.

In many cases, it is absolutely necessary for one to be in close contact with, and under the instruction of a pastor or elder in order to not only obtain a healing, but to remain healed or delivered. This does not mean that only elders are allowed to pray for the sick for all believers can do this. However, although the commission to lay hands upon the sick is given to the believer (Mark 16:15, 18), it would be wise to know and discern who it is that is ministering any of the gifts of the Holy Spirit. One can impart either blessing or cursing with his mouth and also with the laying on of hands.

It is far more preferable to receive ministry from one who is flowing with the Lord and who is not in any kind of rebellion— that is, one who is rightly related to the Lord and to the authority within the body of Christ. Those who would minister in the setting of a church meeting should take note that the pastor or elder in charge of the meeting is the one who holds the responsibility for what goes on. All ministry should submit to his authority, participating or not participating according to his leadership and discernment of what is appropriate. This is of particular importance when visitors in the meeting desire to exercise their gifts. "Know them which labor among you" (1 Thess. 5:12 KJV).

Sometimes when ministering to the sick, physical healings can occur immediately in a spectacular display of the power and love of God. On one such occasion while at Tennessee-Georgia Christian Camp, Evelyn and I prayed for a boy with a withered hand which was about half the size of his other hand. While his mother stood behind him, we prayed, and his hand started to grow out right before our eyes. How excited we were to see this immediate answer to our prayers!

At that meeting we also prayed for a woman who had one foot which was size five and a half, the other foot was size eight and her underdeveloped foot began to grow as we prayed. It was there that the Lord told me that he was teaching my hands to war. Since then, I've used my hands in battle against many kinds of infirmities and against the work of the enemy (Ps. 18:34), all in the name of Jesus Christ our Lord.

On another occasion in Key West, when we prayed for a man who was born blind in one eye, he could see through that eye immediately. There we also prayed for a woman to be healed of a tremendous bloating of her abdomen. The following day she went to see her pastor and he reported to us that the woman's dress was already beginning to hang in folds as the bloating went down.

Jesus only did what He was directed to do by the Father (John 5:30) and He always ministered effectively. With that in mind, we have this confidence: if we pray for a sick person because the Lord has told us to, then he will be healed whether healing comes immediately or slowly. Those who minister must know, as Jesus knew, that they are beloved of the Father; that they are sent by Him to heal the afflicted and set the captives free; that they have that same power of the Holy Spirit in them as did Jesus; that they are not only appointed by God, but that they are anointed by God, to preach the Good News to the downtrodden; that they do nothing of their own will but have come to do the will of Him who sends them. Then they can have the boldness to venture out and believe that they are empowered by God and that God will perform His Word.

Sometimes the Lord will give us an exterior witness that we are moving in His will. Early in our life as born-again Christians, Evelyn and I went to the hospital to pray for a dying woman. As we knelt by the side of her bed holding hands and praying, an electric current went up my legs through my body and into my arms. I knew that the woman was healed! I got up from my knees and ran out of the room, crying. Evelyn followed me and asked me what was wrong. I answered, "She is healed!" There was no evidence that she was healed, but I knew that she was. I was deeply moved because God had given me a sign. She was discharged from the hospital within the week.

Many times after that I would feel the same electricity through my body as I prayed for someone, and I would know that the person was healed. Then, the sign was gone—no more electric current, although people were still being healed when I prayed for them. I wondered why. The Lord told me one day, "Signs are for babies and it is time for you to grow up." There are still occasions when I look for a sign in order to be sure that I'm doing the right thing, but I know that the Lord wants me to mature and to walk by faith rather than by sight.

The Lord has given us many assurances of His abundant provision for us as His children. Sadly, many Christians have unnecessarily postponed the healing of their bodies to the time when the Lord returns and have resigned themselves to carry their burdens throughout this life. Proverbs 13:12 tells us that, "hope deferred makes the heart sick, but desire fulfilled is a tree of life." We have seen this truth illustrated many times, not only by those who have no hope of being made whole in this life, but also by those whose youthful dreams of love, adventure, recognition, security, and success have been for the most part unfulfilled. They have yet to realize that if they would delight themselves in the Lord, He would give them the desire of their hearts (Ps. 37:4). The minister who brings healing to the sick of body and to the sick of heart must immerse those people in the Word and stir up in them a hopeful expectation that God will meet their needs.

4. *Healing Through Deliverance*

The fourth type of healing is healing from illnesses caused by demonic affliction. A classic example of this can be seen in Luke 13:11-13, 16:

> And behold, there was a woman who for eighteen years had had a sickness caused by a spirit; and she was bent double, and could not straighten up at all. And when Jesus saw her, He called her over and said to her, "Woman, you are freed from your sickness." And He laid His hands upon her; and immediately she was made erect again, and began glorifying God . . ." And this woman, a daughter of Abraham as she is, whom Satan has bound for eighteen long years, should she not have been released from this bond on the Sabbath day?

The minister of healing must view every need from God's perspective, seeking the Lord for His understanding and wisdom in matters such as these. Proverbs 3:18 describes the wisdom of God as a tree of life to those who have it. It is with this wisdom that we can effectively deal with the enemy.

Once while ministering in a church in central Florida I prayed for a man who complained of feeling crippled. I commanded a crippling spirit to leave him in the name of Jesus. As soon as I said those words, his body became contorted and he had the appearance of being terribly crippled. No doubt, that spirit was demonstrating its power over him and portraying the eventual condition of the man if it were allowed to remain. We commanded that spirit out of him, prayed for him to be healed, and he was set free. The man was delighted and ran back into the meeting excitedly proclaiming that the Lord had worked and he was healed. All traces of pain and crippling were gone.

As unbelievable as it may seem, there are those who intentionally block their own healing. They do not want to be healed because they enjoy being sick. When Jesus spoke to the lame man at the pool of Bethesda, He asked the man if he wanted to be healed (John 5:6). Perhaps the lame man had never before faced that decision. His response to Jesus was in the affirmative.

This was not the case when Evelyn and I tried to minister to a pretty twenty-two-year-old blind girl who had been afflicted by a spirit of blindness. When we came against it, the spirit spoke out of her declaring that it didn't have to leave because the girl wanted to be blind. She enjoyed all the attention and service bestowed upon her and did not want the responsibilities of a sighted person. I did not want to take the demon's word for it, so I asked the girl if she wanted to be healed. She answererd, "No." Therefore, there was nothing we could do to help her. She had made her decision.

Wisdom directs us not to wear ourselves out on such individuals but to expend our energies on those who honestly desire to walk in the fullness of the Lord's provision. We pray that in time those who have no desire to be well will recognize how foolish and selfish they are and repent.

Some earnestly seek the Lord for release from their physical afflictions but, as yet, have not been healed. Discernment will show us how to pray and obtain the healing for many of them; however, we do not pretend to have all the answers to the problem of why some are not healed. Nevertheless, we pray for those who ask, just as the Lord did in His earthly ministry, trusting Him that He will perform His Word and leaving the responsibility for His Word with Him. We know that no one who trusts God will ever be disappointed.

At the end of the age when all things have been revealed to His saints, then we will fully appreciate, understand, and freely partake of that tree of life with its leaves which are for the healing of the nations. Deep within our hearts there is a yearning for that day when all will be set into order, when the original fallen creation has passed away, and we hear the voice from the throne saying:

> "Behold, the tabernacle of God is among men, and He shall dwell among them, and they shall be His peoples, and God Himself shall be among them, and He shall wipe away every tear from their eyes; and there shall no longer be any death; there shall no longer be any mourning, or crying, or pain; the first things have passed away." And He who sits on the throne said, "Behold, I am making all things new." And He said, "Write, for these words are faithful and true." (Rev. 21:3-5)

SEVEN
HOW TO KEEP
YOUR HEALING
AND DELIVERANCE

Once a healing or deliverance is experienced, the believer may think that that is the end of the story. However, in many instances the believer finds that he is soon engaged in a battle to keep this victory secured—perhaps an even fiercer battle than the one in which he obtained his healing and deliverance in the first place. We offer to the reader fifteen defenses which will enable him to safeguard the provision with which God has blessed him.

1. *Put on the Whole Armor of God.* (Eph. 6:10-18)
   Paul prefaces his description of the armor of God by exhorting the believer to be strong in the strength of God's might. He explains that God's purpose for the armor is to enable us to stand firm against the schemes of the devil. He further notes that we are not really in conflict against people but against spiritual forces of wickedness. We are to equip ourselves with God's full armor even though at present we may not be embattled. Paul warns us that we need advance preparation in order to be able to resist the enemy whenever he does attack us. Afer we have done all this, then we can stand firmly and securely.

   The believer's stance should be one of vigilance against a crafty enemy. Each element mentioned in Ephesians 6 constitutes a portion of our provision. If we neglect any part of it, we leave ourselves open to being wounded and overcome. We are indeed battling against principalities and powers. Satan is God's archenemy who seeks to bring absolute ruin not only upon us but upon the kingdom of God. It is foolishness to think that one can choose not to enter into battle with a foe that is grimly determined to bring us all down to hell if he can. Let us examine each part of our defense system and see how God wants us to use it.

a. Stand firm therefore (v. 14)

Hold your ground now that you have prepared yourself for battle. We are not told to march against the enemy but to stand. The battle is already won. Jesus Christ is the victor and we stand firm on the ground that is His. We do not fight as if trying to gain the ground for we already have it. We fight as victors who are determined to hold the ground that has been obtained for us by the blood of Jesus. It is in the strength of this position of ownership that we can repel any intruders.

b. Having girded your loins with truth (v. 14)

Here the believer is encircled with the truth of God's Word that will prevent him from falling into error, unreality, deception, illusions, and perversion. There is a difference between what is *true* and what is *truth*. For example, while it is "true" that Jesus suffered a humiliating torturous death at Calvary, the *truth* is that by His very death and apparent defeat on the cross, He won the victory over sin and death, and is alive forevermore. Hallelujah!

Many a deception has been effected by a person merely telling what is *true* in such a way as to hide the *truth* from being known. Gossip often has this quality about it, and so do prejudice and feuds. Lying spirits will try to engage our minds in consideration about how weak and ineffective we are against temptation, how we must wait for "another day" to be healed or delivered. Indeed, we are no longer certain any more that God really accepts us since we fall into sin so often. Down, down, down, go our defenses once we lose sight of the truth of our salvation. The *truth* is that we are accepted in the Beloved; that Jesus paid the price once for all of our sins for all time and that it is by grace through faith tht we ever receive redemption, healing, deliverance, or anything else from God. In his second letter to the Corinthians 6:1-3, Paul urges us not to receive the grace of God in vain—"Behold, now is the day of salvation."

c. And having put on the breastplate of righteousness (v. 14)

The breastplate protects the heart and vital organs of the body. If we are unrighteous in our ways before God, or in our dealings with other people, or in our secret thoughts and motives, we leave ourselves wide open to evil invading our heart. Then, corruption can develop swiftly both in the physical and spiritual realms. In this vulnerable condition without the breastplate of righteousness, any deliverance or healing which we have received from God can be lost. We dare not depend upon our own good works but must put on the righteousness of Christ by whose shed blood we have become righteous.

d. And having shod your feet with the preparation of the gospel of peace (v. 15)

The gospel is a positive proclamation rather than being a negative prohibitive word.

> How lovely on the mountains
> Are the feet of him who brings good news,
> Who announces peace
> And brings good news of happiness,
> Who announces salvation,
> And says to Zion, "Your God reigns!" (Isa. 52:7)

Our feet must be shod with preparedness to proclaim that joyful message to all who we encounter, both friend and foe, as we go through life.

e. In addition to all, taking up the shield of faith (v. 16)

Paul tells us that this shield will enable us to extinguish all the flaming missiles of the evil one. Faith enables us to see the devil as defeated; faith enables us to praise God as having already won for Himself and for us the victory in every situation of life. When the evil one shoots us a fiery dart, faith tells us that we are saved by God's grace; that Jesus is Lord; that we are accepted in the beloved; that God indwells us by His Spirit. Faith puts out that fire and doubt is extinguished.

f. And take the helmet of salvation (v. 17)

The helmet of salvation gives us protection against all the mental attacks of Satan. When we are secure in the knowledge that we are saved by the blood of Jesus, that we are part of the household of God, that He is our Father and we are joint-heirs with Christ, we can peacefully rest in His love and successfully ward off any doubts, fears and temptations. Then, we are empowered to bring into captivity every thought to the obedience of Christ. Make no mistake about it—we are dealing with a superior enemy who can naturally outthink us at every turn. We cannot devise an effective defense against him by our own human ingenuity. The only way we can win is by the provision of God's wisdom, discernment, and knowledge.

g. And the sword of the Spirit, which is the word of God (v. 17)

The armor of God is not to be worn with the detached stoicism of the uninvolved; rather, it can be effective only when the believer, as a combatant, wields his weapon. God has placed the sword of the Spirit at our disposal and He expects us to use it well. One who is unskilled with a sword would never enter a match against a practiced opponent with any hope of victory. How foolish we are when we allow our weapon to sit upon a shelf gathering dust instead of using it daily to gain knowledge, assurance, strength, wisdom, courage, hope, and faith. Our increased facility with the Word of God will be demonstrated whenever our position in Christ is challenged. Out of the depths of our being we will be able to speak a word which will pierce through the enemy's facade of strength and he will flee before us. It is the specific word which God gives us each time we are challenged that will be effective, just as Jesus responded to and effectively dealt with Satan when he tempted Jesus in the wilderness (Matt. 4:1-11).

h. With all prayer and petition pray at all times in the Spirit, and with this in view, be on the alert with all perseverance and petition for all the saints. (v. 18)

The believer cannot separate himself from the body of Christ. As a member of the Church Vigilant he is obliged not only to do battle, praying as the Holy Spirit directs, for himself but also to intercede on behalf of his brothers and sisters in Christ with the same determination.

2. *Know Your Position in Christ*

Then he showed me Joshua the high priest standing before the angel of the Lord and Satan standing at his right hand to accuse him. And the Lord said to Satan, "The Lord rebuke you, Satan! Indeed, the Lord who has chosen Jerusalem rebuke you! Is this not a brand plucked from the fire?" Now Joshua was clothed with filthy garments and standing before the angel." (Zech. 3:1-3)

Then the Lord directed that the filthy garments be removed from Joshua and that he be clothed with festal robes and given a clean turban for his head. In response to the accusations of Satan that we are not worthy to receive any blessing from God, we must see ourselves in the same position as Joshua, as brands which the Lord has plucked out of the fire and as those clothed in the clean robes of righteousness. The same admonishment which the angel gives to Joshua applies to us also if we desire to have authority over the enemy and unlimited fellowship within the household of God:

"Thus says the Lord of hosts, 'If you will walk in My ways, and if you will perform My service, then you will also govern My house and also have charge of My courts, and I will grant you free access among these who are standing here." (Zech. 3:7)

3. *Make a Positive Confession*

There is a very close tie between what we believe and what we profess or confess with our mouth.

"The word is near you, in your mouth and in your heart"—that is, the word of faith which we are preaching, that if you confess with your mouth Jesus as Lord, and believe in your heart that God raised Him from the dead, you shall be saved; for with the heart man believes, resulting in righteousness, and with the mouth he confesses resulting in salvation. (Rom. 10:8-10)

This principle is universally true and will affect not only what we state but also what we do. If we believe that the train will run over us unless we get off the tracks, we will not only shout a warning to everyone who stands in the path of the oncoming train, but we will leap to safety. If we believe that by the flogging which Jesus suffered we have been healed, we will not only proclaim that good news to all but we will begin thanking and praising God for His wonderful provision with joyful hearts, expecting to see that provision manifested in our bodies. Jesus describes the power we have in this combination of faith and declaration:

> "Truly I say to you, whoever says to this mountain, 'Be taken up and cast into the sea,' and does not doubt in his heart, but believes that what he says is going to happen; it shall be granted him. Therefore I say to you, all things for which you pray and ask, believe that you have received them, and they shall be granted you." (Mark 11:23-24)

Here we must take our direction from the Holy Spirit who will guide us in when and how to apply the Scriptures to each situation just as Jesus was directed moment by moment by His Father (John 5:19).

4. Deal Promptly With Sin

The longer we postpone seeking to become holy, the longer we will delay much of God's blessings from reaching us. Often, illness will reoccur or an exorcised evil spirit will return as a direct result of a person's failing to deal with sin in his life.

> But your iniquities have made a separation between you and your God, and your sins have hid His face from you, so that He does not hear. (Isa. 59:2)

5. Stay in the Word of God

God's Word is both the standard for us to live by (Josh. 1:8) and nourishment to strengthen and enable us to live according to that standard (Ps. 1:1-3). "Thy words were found and I ate them, and Thy words became for me a joy and the delight of my heart; for I have been called by Thy name, O Lord God of hosts (Jer. 15:16). God reveals himself, His ways and His will in His Word. Many blessings are missed or lost simply because of ignorance of the Scriptures. May we hunger more for spiritual bread than for the food that we stuff into our stomachs!

6. *Forgive*

In the Lord's Prayer, we first recognize who God is and we commit our wills over to Him and His kingdom. Next, we make three requests of Him: first, that He would feed us daily; second, that He would forgive us in the same manner that we forgive others; and third, rather than leading us into temptation, He, instead, would deliver us out of the hand of the evil one. How often have we prayed that prayer just mumbling the words without comprehending what we were saying. We cannot declare God as sovereign ruler of the heavens without acknowledging Him as King of all on earth—the absolute ruler of everything He has created. We cannot call Him "Lord" and, at the same time, withhold from Him any portion of our lives, private or interpersonal. We cannot say to Him, "Forgive me, Lord," while holding a grudge against our brother. If we try to ignore or omit parts of the prayer, we nullify the whole prayer. God, who would be our refuge and our strength, who would feed us and care for us, keeping us safe from the power of the enemy, will no longer do so for we actually ask Him not to by our words: "Forgive us our debts as we forgive our debtors." When Jesus told Peter that he should forgive his brother up to seventy times seven, He was not recommending that Peter keep a record of offenses. Rather, Jesus was indicating that forgiveness was to be freely given without measure. When God forgives us, He no longer remembers our sin (Heb. 10:17). We are required to extend the same attitude of mercy to others if we desire God to be merciful to us. Jesus' story about the slave whose master forgave him his debt but who was unwilling to forgive the debt owed to him by his fellow-slave has a chilling conclusion:

> "Then summoning him, his lord said to him, 'You wicked slave, I forgave you all that debt because you entreated me. Should you not also have had mercy on your fellow-slave, even as I had mercy on you?' And his lord, moved with anger, handed him over to the torturers until he should repay all that was owed him. So shall My heavenly Father also do to you, if each of you does not forgive his brother from your heart." (Matt. 18:32-35)

7. *Crucify the Flesh*

> Now those who belong to Christ Jesus have crucified the flesh with its passions and desires. If we live by the Spirit, let us also walk by the Spirit. (Gal. 5:24-25)

We who belong to Christ are united with Him in His death on the cross and in His resurrection to eternal life for the purpose of ending the power that sin and death once had over us. We are exhorted by Paul in Romans 6 to consider ourselves dead to sin but alive to God, to not let sin reign in our mortal bodies, and to present our physical bodies to God as weapons of righteousness for His purposes. Oftentimes, a brother will not be able to receive or keep a healing because he is nurturing his flesh, that is, his carnal unredeemed mind and bodily appetites. He is living according to his willful sensual nature on the level of the instincts and, therefore, cannot please God (Rom. 8:7, 8). This kind of existence, will bring certain death to his spiritual life. Falling away from the crucified life can occur very subtly, and the self-deceived brother may not even realize that he is compromising in this way. Paul's question would bring the erring believer back to reality:

> Do you not know that when you present yourselves to someone as slaves for obedience, you are slaves of the one whom you obey, either of sin resulting in death, or of obedience resulting in righteousness? (Rom. 6:16)

Just in case the reader would still miss the point and exclude himself from having any fleshly drives, Paul gives us a partial list of activities of the flesh in Galatians 5:19. Along with such things as orgies, witchcraft, sexual immorality, and worship of false gods, which we would obviously renounce, he also includes some things which the average Christian might not consider to be in the same category of sin: impurity of mind, sensuality, hatred, strife, jealousy, bad temper, rivalry, factions, party-spirit, envy, drunkenness "and things like these." Contrary to God's standard, we often set for ourselves our own standard for holiness and are often comfortable with practices which God detests.

8. & 9. *Praise and Thanksgiving*

It is God's will that in all of life's situations we would be expressive of our gratitude and praise toward Him (1 Thess. 5:18). It is only in that frame of mind, that attitude of heart, that we can be blessed. If we grumble and complain, we identify ourselves with the children of Israel who wandered through the desert for forty years and were not allowed to enter into the rest of God. Their grumblings, and ours also, clearly demonstrate unbelief, and without faith it is impossible to please God (Heb. 11:6). David leads us into the presence of the Lord with the joyful words of Psalm 100. As we draw near to Him who loves us, let us proclaim His lovingkindness and faithfulness with grateful hearts. Let this attitude spill over into our relationships with others where we all too often fail to show appreciation.

10. *Fellowship*

Separatism and independence are not healthy characteristics within the body of Christ. Whether we like it or not, we are as much a part of each other as we are a part of Jesus. "The eye cannot say to the hand, 'I have no need of you'" (1 Cor. 12:21). Since we limit or expand the depth of our fellowhip with Jesus by the same measure that we limit or expand our relationships with each other, we dare not interpose any further doctrinal requirements on each other beyond the fundamental precepts of our faith; nor dare we establish any other standard for our loving acceptance of each other than the standard by which Jesus lovingly accepts us.

> There should be no division in the body, but that the members should have the same care for one another. And if one member suffers, all the members suffer with it; if one member is honored, all the members rejoice with it. Now you are Christ's body and individually members of it. (1 Cor. 12:25-27)

If we can capture the vision of the many different Christian denominations as being essential organs and limbs of the body of Christ; if we can see individual Christians as having the same cellular identity as Jesus, the head of the body; and if we can see ourselves linked together in a vital life-flow with every other part, then, we will truly recognize the body of Christ for what it is. We must remember that Paul explained to the Corinthian church that not discerning the body rightly was the reason that many of them had become sick, weak, and had even died prematurely (1 Cor. 11:30). We cannot afford to go our own way, but we should encourage one another to love and to do good deeds and not forsake the assembling of ourselves together (Heb. 10:24, 25). United, we are a powerful force against the works of darkness. Divided, we are weak and ineffective.

> And if one can overpower him who is alone, two can resist him. A cord of three strands is not quickly torn apart. (Eccles. 4:12)

11. *Submit to Authority*

Authority in the church seems to have three legitimate areas of scope:
1. Corporate life
   a. oversight in those ministries and activities that are done in the name of the congregation or parish
   b. providing for a time and place of common worship and instruction in the Word
   c. developing new ministries from among the people, giving each opportunities to serve and to express the gift of God within them
2. Assistance in establishing Christ as the head of every family unit, offering teaching and counseling wherever there is a need
3. Outreach—evangelism
   a. bringing new believers into relationship with the Lord and with other members of the congregation
   b. gathering in the "lost sheep," the unchurched, who have no sustaining church life.

With this in mind, in his open letter to the Church which is scattered throughout the civilized world, Peter exhorts the elders to shepherd the flock of God unselfishly, not by lording it over the people, but by being examples to the flock (1 Pet. 5:1-4). Also he instructs the younger men to be subject to their elders. Paul deals with this issue in Hebrews 13:17 instructing the believers to obey those leaders who keep watch over their souls and will have to give an accounting to God for whatever leadership they provide. On the other hand, Paul speaks harshly about Diotrephes who "wants to be head of everything" (as he is described in 3 John 9, 10, J.B. Phillips New Testament). He stands in stark contrast with Jesus who washed His followers' feet and told them that He who would be the greatest among them must be the servant of all.

Peaceful relationships within the framework of ecclesiastical authority can be summed up by 1 Pet. 5:5: "All of you, clothe yourselves with humility toward one another, for God is opposed to the proud, but gives grace to the humble."

12. *Cultivate the Fruit of the Holy Spirit*

Galatians 5 describes the struggle that goes on within each of us between the deeds of the flesh and the fruit of the Spirit. We, as the children of God, should fervently desire to walk in the Spirit, no longer to be ruled by the passions and desires of the flesh. We can be confident that this is an obtainable goal because the Word of God commands us to walk in the Spirit and not in the flesh, and God does not command us to do the impossible. What then must we do in order to see the fruit of the Holy Spirit abound in our lives and to sensitively know and do all that He leads us to do?

a. Love the Lord our God withour whole mind and heart . . . and love your neighbor as yourselves. (Mark 12:30, 31)
b. Offer our bodies as a living and holy sacrifice. (Rom. 12:1)
c. Submit our wills to God. (John 5:30)
d. Set your affection on the heavenly, not the earthly. (Col. 3:2)
e. Be filled with the Spirit, speaking to yourselves in Psalms and hymns. (Eph. 5:18, 19)
f. Trust God to work in us both to will and to do His good pleasure. (Phil. 2:13)
g. Humble ourselves under the mighty hand of God. (1 Pet. 5:6)

13. *Get Homelife in Order*

Whatever and whoever we truly are, we will demonstrate it in our homes when no visitors are there to observe. This is where our Christianity is proven. This is where the inner person is revealed. That is why those who would minister and serve publicly in the church must be first examined as to the quality of their homelife (1 Tim. 3:3-13) for we minister out of the spirit of our homes.

Immediately following these words in Ephesians 5:18-20: "Be filled with the Spirit, speaking to one another in psalms and hymns and spiritual songs, singing and making melody with your heart to the Lord; always giving thanks for all things in the name of our Lord Jesus Christ to God even the Father;" we read: "And be subject to one another in the fear of Christ" (v. 21). Then comes the well-known passage of instructions to wives directing them to submit themselves to their husbands, to husbands to lay down their lives for their wives, to children to obey their parents, and to fathers to bring their children up in the fear and discipline of the Lord (Eph. 5:22-33 and 6:1-4). The verses which precede this passage are not there by accident. Being filled with the Spirit, speaking to one another in psalms and hymns and making melody with your heart to the Lord, of necessity, must precede any efforts to live together successfully in proper order. This places the emphasis upon attitude rather than actions and gives the Spirit of God preeminence in our closest relationships (those which are most often abused). When these are holy, we give no opportunity to the enemy to invade our homes with strife, pain, misery.

14. *Pray Always*

a. Worship and Fellowship with God—When we are in the same room with another person, we are usually very aware of that fact. We converse with him not only verbally but also nonverbally. With our eyes, hands, and movements, etc., we communicate our awareness of his presence. If we ignore or neglect to recognize that he is with us, we will communicate our lack of esteem for him. The same is true in our relationship with God who is ever present. Our prayer life or lack of it will have a direct bearing upon the fellowship we have with God and upon the strength of our whole being as our fellowship with Him matures.

b. Petition and Intercession—Prayer is not a means by which we achieve our aims. If our motive in praying is to get our own way in a matter, we will fail miserably (James 4:3). Before we pray, we should determine what is the will of God and pray according to His will. Then He will hear our prayers and we will have what we have asked of Him (1 John 5:14, 15). There are times when we simply do not know how to pray. Then we can pray in tongues.

> And in the same way the Spirit also helps our weakness; for we do not know how to pray as we should, but the Spirit Himself intercedes for us with groanings too deep for words; and He who searches the hearts knows what the mind of the Spirit is, because He intercedes for the saints according to the will of God. (Rom. 8:26, 27)

Also, we find that praying in an unknown tongue has an edifying effect upon the inner person (1 Cor. 14:2-4). One who is built up in his spirit will be more able to withstand the attacks of the enemy and more able to keep his healing and deliverance.

15. *Total Commitment*

Webster defines "total" as "complete" and "entire." He defines "commitment" as "the delivery of a person or thing into the charge or keeping of another." How total is our commitment to God? Our sincerity is demonstrated not only by how well we relate to others, but, perhaps, can best be evaluated by observing how we hold our resources of time, energy, and money. If all these are completely given over to God then we may consider ourselves well on the way to total commitment. Whatever we hold onto as our own will ultimately come between us and the Lord.

> We should serve the Lord not only because He is God and because he is worthy, but also because it is in our best interest to do so. "And now, Israel, what does the Lord your God require from you, but to fear the Lord your God, to walk in all His ways and love Him, and to serve the Lord your God with all your heart and with all your soul, and to keep the Lord's commandments and His statutes which I am commanding you today for your good?" (Deut. 10:12, 13)

We who serve the Lord find that as we grow in holiness—that is, complete separation from the world unto God—the greater becomes our joy. God must be the center of our existence, not ourselves, our pursuits, our preferences, our families, or anything else. It is all or nothing where God is concerned. He will accept nothing less than our total commitment, and that is for our own good.

Appendix

A. *Pre-counseling requirements for ministers*
   1. Be baptized in the Holy Spirit.
   2. Go through deliverance yourself.
   3. Learn how to minister in the gifts of the Spirit.
   4. Have a servant's heart.
   5. Be uncompromising with the enemy.
   6. Be certain that God has called you to this ministry.
   7. Have true compassion (not human sympathy) for the counselee—guard against developing a judgmental or self-righteous attitude.
   8. Have a listening ear.
   9. Be flexible in a variety of techniques.
   10. Search for root causes in the counselee's problems.
   11. Use the sword of the Spirit—not your own human resources.
   12. Believe not every spirit—evil spirits will lie to you.
   13. Be able to diagnose the problem—flesh or spirit.
   14. Be prepared to confront counselee with his personal responsibility.

B. *Counselor's Checklist for Success*
   1. Don't use cliches or pat answers; i.e., "I know just how you feel." "Just give yourself to Jesus." Some don't know how to surrender their lives to Jesus. If they did, they wouldn't be needing counseling.
   2. Don't feel that you have to come up with an answer for everything. If you don't know, say so, but tell the counselee that you will try to find out.
   3. Don't try to cast out every demon in the world or try to cover too much in one session. (Keep each session under two hours if possible.)
   4. Don't wear yourself out or wear out the counselee.
   5. Don't become a permanent crutch. Teach the counselee self-deliverance and the overcoming life.
   6. Don't advise anything contrary to Scripture.
   7. Don't advise anything that would be presuming on God; i.e., take off your glasses, give up medicine, etc.

8. Don't discuss the counselee with others.

9 Don't counsel alone in a private place with a member of the opposite sex.

10. Be very careful of physical contact.

11. Don't be sloppy in your personal appearance, manner, grooming, cleanliness. Be professional.

12. Don't minister if you are tired.

13. Don't think that you cannot fall or need further deliverance yourself.

C. *Why Some Counselors Fail*

1. Immaturity and/or inexperience—unskilled in the Word.

2. Counselor's personal problems—smoking, lust, pride, etc.

3. Inadequate prayer and fasting.

4. Failure to dig for root causes.

5. Counselor becoming emotionally involved.

6. Pride in either counselor or counselee.

7. Counselor's desire to have control over others.

8. Similar weakness in counselor.

9. Failure to check for proper foundations in life of counselee: salvation, baptism, relationships.

10. Failure to discern natural causes for problem.

11. Lack of desperation on part of counselee—not willing to give up all for Jesus or to obey.

12. Counselee does not take personal responsibility for his condition or actions.

CASSETTE TAPES BY EVANGELIST FRANK MARZULLO

HEALING & DELIVERANCE SERIES

1. Diagnosing the Problem
2. Discerning of Spirits
3. Deliverance
4. Doublemindedness
5. Total Healing
6. How to Keep Your Healing

OTHER DELIVERANCE TAPES

Children Deliverance
Blessings and Curses
Soul Ties and Occultism
Do's & Don'ts for Deliverance
Instructions for Deliverance

SPIRITUAL WARFARE SERIES

Casting Out Unclean Spirits #1
Casting Out Unclean Spirits #2
Winning the Spiritual Battle
1. Fighting the Spiritual Battle
2. Bondage or Freedom
3. Binding the Strong Man
4. Freedom From Bondage to Man

OVERCOMING LIFE SERIES

1. Dying to Self
2. Power in the Spoken Word
3. Power in the Blood of Jesus
4. Battle for Your Mind

SPANISH TAPES

Quien Me Ha Tocado?
Fe Positivo Y Negativo
Y Por Cuanto Sois Hijos
Ser un Brazo de Dios
El Poder de la Palabra
Creciendo en el Senor

OTHER TAPES

Have You Ever Failed?
Highway to Holiness
Pressing on to Maturity
Working in the Power of God
Getting Rid of Worry
Fear . . . Obstacle to Faith

HOLY SPIRIT SERIES (GIFTS)

Tongues & Interpretation
Prophecy
Discerning of Spirits
Word of Knowledge & Wisdom
Miracles, Faith, Healings

RECENT TAPES

Be a Channel of God
Because Ye Are Sons
Negative and Positive Faith
There Is a Way Out

HEALING TAPES

Removing the Mountain
I Am the Lord That Heals Thee
God's Healing Plan for You
Healing the Broken Heart & Spirit
Divine Order in Your Family

SPANISH DELIVERANCE TAPES

Liberacion #1
Liberacion #2
Como Ganar la Batalia Espirit
Atando al Hombre Fuerte
Taller de Obreros de Liberation

*(Each Cassette Tape
$4.00 Donation)*

Other Books by Evangelist Frank Marzullo

*EIGHT KEYS TO SPIRITUAL AND
PHYSICAL HEALTH . . . . Donation $5.00

Spanish Version of Above:
LLAVES PARA MINISTRAR LIBERACION
Y SANIDAD . . . . Donation $5.00

---

*DYING TO SELF . . . . Donation $2.00

*POWER IN THE SPOKEN WORD . . . . Donation $2.00

*POWER IN THE BLOOD OF JESUS . . Donation $2.00

*BATTLE FOR YOUR MIND . . . . Donation $2.00

*SOUND MIND, NOT FEAR . . . . Donation $2.00

*HEALING OF THE BROKEN HEART AND THE
WOUNDED SPIRIT . . . . Donation $2.00

**ALL CASSETTE TAPES . . . . Donation $4.00
(Page 94)**

Please add $1.00 for postage/handling
Make checks payable to "Christian Covenant Fellowship"

SEND REQUEST TO

EVANGELIST FRANK MARZULLO
1510 W. STEVENS AVENUE
DELAND, FLORIDA 32720
(904) 738-0036